BACCHUS & ME

Books by Jay McInerney

BACCHUS & ME

ADVENTURES IN THE WINE CELLAR

JAY MCINERNEY

THE LYONS PRESS

Printed in Canada

Designed by Compset, Inc.

All but one of these articles have previously appeared in
House & Garden magazine in the column "Uncorked"; one
article appeared in *The New Yorker*.

10 9 8 7 6 5 4 3 2 1

Library of Congress Cataloging-in-Publication Data

McInerney, Jay.
Bacchus & me: adventures in the wine cellar / Jay McInerney.
     p. cm.
      ISBN 1-58574-186-8
      1. Wine and wine making.   I. Title: Bacchus and me.
     II. Title.
TP548.M4675 2000
641.2'2—dc21

00-62164

For Dominique Browning

CONTENTS

INTRODUCTION

This wine critic gig began as a form of moonlighting. On my passport it says I'm a novelist, and my previous books have all been works of fiction. I've had daydreams about accepting the Nobel prize for literature since I was seventeen; until recently I never really imagined myself standing in a cellar of Château Lafite at ten in the morning tasting the new vintage out of barrel, let alone publishing a book about wine.

It all started about five years ago with a phone call from Dominique Browning, an old friend who'd recently been given the mandate of resurrecting *House & Garden,* the venerable Condé Nast shelter journal. In her wisdom, which runs pretty deep, Dominique decided that in the new post–tuna-casserole America, she wanted to cover wine as well as food, couches, and nasturtiums. And apparently she decided that it would be fun to hire an enthusiast who was not necessarily a specialist.

Those assembled at one of the early staff meetings liked the idea. However, when the concept was fleshed out with my name, I'm told that eyebrows were raised, while jaws and even pins were dropped. The feeling seems to have been that I had made my name, such as it was, by writing about people who abused controlled substances and ravaged their nasal passages. (See *Bright Lights, Big City,* Vintage, 1984.) What the hell did I know about wine?

Good question. As Dominique pointed out, I knew a little more than might be expected. As a friend she was aware of the fact that I had suffered a mild and relatively benign case of oenophilia for years. I was a collector and a drinker, a reader of wine journals and wine catalogues. And a talker. In providing an outlet for my passion she may have been thinking of our mutual friends, some of whom were possibly getting tired of listening to me hold forth on the subject.

My only formal credential in the wine trade was my year of employment at the Westcott Cordial Shop in Syracuse, New York. I worked as a clerk for minimum wage while studying writing with Raymond Carver and writing my first novel. The neighborhood was a marginal one, situated between the university and the ghetto, and while we displayed bottles of vintage Bordeaux—I specifically remember the bottle of '78 Smith-Haut-Lafitte with its blue and yellow label—they tended to collect dust; much of our trade was in the area of industrially fortified grape juice—selling Wild Irish Rose and Night Train to guys with bad personal hygiene. Still, the proprietor of the shop was a Princeton man who had an extensive wine library on the premises and high hopes for the eventual gentrification of the neighborhood. I used to dip into the wine library between robberies and grad school assignments. And I used to dip into the stock when I left at night, it being the tradition among the clerks to supplement our paltry incomes with the odd bottle of Yugoslavian Cabernet.

I worked my way up from the cheapest bottles of Eastern European table wine—we had quite a few in the two-dollar range—all the way up to the Spanish bubbly, which at that time cost five or six bucks. It wasn't a bad way to learn. Later, after my first novel was published and became a best-seller, I was able to afford some of those vintage Bordeaux. By then I had developed the start of a palate. I certainly knew what bad wine tasted like. In *Between Meals* A. J. Liebling makes the case for starting one's gastronomic apprenticeship near the bottom of the food chain. "If the first requisite for writing well about food is a good appetite," he says, "the second is to put in your apprenticeship as a feeder when you have enough money to pay the check but not enough to produce indifference about the size of the total." The same can be said of wine. The poor man, the budget drinker, is forced to make choices and sacrifices that can only sharpen his discrimination and his appreciation of competing pleasures. Starting at the top, one will miss out on the climb.

Perhaps the most significant event in my continuing education as an oenophile took place under strictly literary auspices: Having quit the liquor store a year before, I was in London for the English publication of *Bright Lights, Big City*, where my English editor threw a party for me. Among the many people I met that night was the English novelist Julian Barnes, whose brilliant novel *Flaubert's Parrot* I had just read and admired. I can't quite remember how it was that he came to invite me to dinner—Julian is not the kind of guy who indiscriminately spews invitations—but a few nights later I found myself chez Barnes. Perhaps we had discussed wine at the party—when I arrived he had decanted two bottles of what I would later realize were two legendary Châteauneuf-du-Papes, the '62 and the '67 Jaboulet Les Cedres. I didn't have much respect for Châteauneuf at the time, perhaps because it was the red wine I had first learned to appreciate when I was in college. By then I thought of it as a beginner's wine. As soon as I tasted the '67 I realized I had a lot to learn.

Julian was a year or two ahead of me in terms of his vinous education and his collecting—already he had a pretty significant cellar, composed mainly of clarets (as our Tea-bag friends call the red wines of Bordeaux) and Rhônes. Subsequently I realized that drinking with Julian was like playing tennis with a slightly superior player—in fact he was a superior tennis player as well—the best possible way to learn and to sharpen your game.

My nascent friendship with Julian coincided with the invention of the fax machine. He had one—odd, given what a technophobe he is, that he beat me to it—and I soon acquired one. Being writers, we both distrusted the telephone but found this new medium—meditated and written, yet instant—to be congenial. In between my visits to London and his to America we began to fax each other regularly. Our correspondence covered many topics—literary gossip, notes on our reading, my own romantic mishaps. But always there was wine. We inevitably shared notes on whatever we had been drinking or buying. And I suppose my faxes to Julian are the ancestors of the columns collected here.

At Julian's table, in addition to meeting some of the most interesting literary figures in England, I also met some serious grape nuts, including Jancis Robinson, the wine critic, and her husband Nick Lander, who then owned my favorite London restaurant and now writes about food. Although Jancis does her best to pretend that she's just another girl who likes to throw back a few glasses of *vino*, her presence at a dinner table definitely raises the level of discourse about wine. Even if you have a crush on her you can't help but learn a little in her company. And reading her books will make you feel you're an expert.

Though I didn't meet him until after I had started writing this column, I have to acknowledge the influence of Robert Parker, the mighty Wine Advocate, who demystified the great French growths and educated—*created* might be the better word—an entire generation of wine enthusiasts. He was the presiding deity in my correspondence with Julian. We may sometimes use him as a foil, delighted to discover some point of disagreement. But he's the man.

Parker, of course, made his name by touting the '82 Bordeaux as the vintage of the century. Despite skepticism in France and England—and in rival wine publications—the market, and general opinion, followed Parker in this assessment. After a bad previous decade, the 1980s turned out to be a golden age for Bordeaux. A series of excellent vintages blessed the region; increased investment and improved technology seemed to further improve the picture, resurrecting many previously moribund properties. As a drinker and a collector I felt fortunate to be coming of age at this moment; while many of the wines I bought then still aren't ready to uncork, I was educating myself as to their eventual evolution by drinking the older vintages, especially with my friends in London. As a resident of the East Coast, I found these wines to be more available, and a better value, than the stuff that was coming out of California.

Bordeaux was my first love as a wine drinker. It's easier to understand than any other French wine region. Which is not to say that it's simple. Clarets age better than any other red wines, acquiring amazing complexity over the years. But they are also more consistent than, say, Burgundies.

I have more Bordeaux in my cellar than any other kind of wine, though I'm not adding much these days. In part this may reflect a slight shift of taste toward the fickle but exquisite pleasures of Burgundy and Pinot Noir. In part it also reflects the fact that the 1990s produced few good vintages in Bordeaux while prices increased inexorably. By the time you read this, the verdict will be in on the vintage of 2000. As one Bordeaux *négotiant* told me, "We desperately need a great vintage." He's right. I will always love claret. But I've learned, especially since I started writing this column, that there are other regions worthy of our respect and attention.

I began this column with something of a prejudice against California wines. They seemed to me to be fairly one dimensional—or at best two dimensional. Ripe, yes. Fruity, yes. So is *Baywatch*. Most seemed to me to lack the complexity and the earthiness of their French and Italian counterparts, as if they had been grown hydroponically. And indeed, until recently, California winemakers didn't think much about what the French call *terroir*. About dirt. In the Napa Valley wine seemed to be treated more like a chemical product than an agricultural product, or so I imagined.

I wasn't entirely wrong. But my objections were already being addressed by a new generation of California winemakers, as I was to discover after I started my column.

One of the people who was dubious about my credentials as a wine columnist was Lora Zarubin—the newly appointed food editor of *House & Garden*. She was only slightly less skeptical after she met me for lunch at the Four Seasons one day. I seem to recall I'd had a rough night and was not, ahem, showing well, as we say of wine when it's at an awkward stage. We have since traveled together through many of the world's wine regions (with Lora's Jack Russell terrier, Bessie) and spent hundreds of pleasurable hours together, but a great friendship did not seem preordained. And while I like to think I impressed her with my general knowledge, she was appalled at my ignorance of California wines. Lora is from San Francisco. A disciple of the great Alice Waters, she had come to New York and opened her own restaurant, which I had patronized, though I'd never met the eponymous proprietor until our prickly lunch at the Four Seasons. Lora decided that if I was going to learn about California wine, I might as well start at the top. She sent me to Helen Turley.

Five years ago Helen Turley was not yet known as the "wine goddess." I'd never heard of her myself. Which was probably a good thing for me. It was as if a fledgling literary critic, on his first assignment, had been dispatched to meet and interview Jane Austen. If I'd really known Helen's stature, and her standards, I would have been terrified. As it was I was pretty anxious driving up the Napa Valley from San Francisco early one morning in order to make our rendezvous in Oakville. It was my absolute first gig as a "professional" wine taster and I was still a little bit put off that Helen had insisted on a ten o'clock tasting. I mean, who the hell drank wine at ten in the morning? (Of course, I knew I was supposed to spit it out—but even that seemed strange. Could one really taste a wine without swallowing it? Damned if I knew.) But Lora had informed me that the taste buds are freshest in the morning and that Helen insisted on showing her wines then. By the time I arrived at the Napa Wine Company I was truly nervous, because I had momentarily forgotten Lora's injunction against drinking coffee before tasting and slugged back an espresso at the Oakville grocery. What's more I was five, no ten, minutes late.

Helen Turley was an impressive figure by any standard. Although we both stand about six feet tall, she seemed much taller to me that morning. She wore a faded work shirt that matched her eyes, her beautiful, just barely kempt mane of blond hair hung well below her shoulders, and she bore an expression that seemed to me to be suspended between warmth and skepticism. She led me into the inner recesses of the Napa Wine Company warehouse, where she was making her wines at the time. Half a dozen huge balloon-shaped Riedel glasses were standing on barrel, awaiting us. Seeing them I suddenly experienced that sickening, loose-boweled feeling I hadn't known in years—the student who is utterly unprepared for his test. And indeed, before I could even taste, Helen was going to quiz me. She started to ask me about my likes and dislikes in wine, and to this day I believe that if my answers hadn't met her approval she might have sent me away without wetting a single glass. I remember only a few of the questions.

"What California wines do you like?" she asked.

Perhaps it was the chill of the warehouse; I found I was shivering. I thought about lying but then I realized I didn't even know the names of that many California wines. "To tell you the truth," I said, "I don't really like many California wines."

For a moment I was afraid I would have to get back in the car and drive back to San Francisco, but this answer didn't seem to offend her. (Later I thought about my friend Buzz Whelker, who taught me to play polo.

When I first explained to him that I'd only been on a horse a few times in my life, he said that was fine by him—he preferred teaching people from scratch rather than having to unteach certain bad riding habits.)

"Do you like any California Chardonnays?" she asked.

"The only one I can remember really liking had a French name," I said. "I think it was called Mon Plaisir. From somebody called Peter Michael."

"Which vintage?"

I named the two recent vintages I had drunk. A few days later I learned that Helen Turley had made those wines.

And once I tasted her '94 Marcassin Chardonnay from barrel—two of the richest, most decadently pleasurable white wines I had ever experienced—I knew I was in the presence of greatness. I went on to taste the spectacular reds Helen was making at that time—the soon-to-be famous Bryant Family and Colgin. I'd never tasted out of barrel before, but Helen seemed at some point to stop judging and begin to encourage me, embroidering my tentative comments and complimenting some of my analogies. I had no idea what I was doing, but Helen decided that I might be worth teaching. Or perhaps she just decided I wasn't worth killing.

Since that nerve-racking morning, I have spent many hours tasting with Helen and many more hours listening to her talk about wine. She and her husband,

John Wetlaufer (with whom I felt an instant kinship—there aren't many of us philosophy majors out there), have taught me more about wine than any single book I've read. (The fact that I remain ignorant of the exact nature of, say, malolactic fermentation should in no way reflect on them.) John was for many years the Napa Valley's leading authority on Burgundy. As the buyer for the All State Wine store in Calistoga, he helped shape and refine the palates of many Napa and Sonoma winemakers. As the quality of Napa and Sonoma wines improves, thanks in no small part to the influence of himself and Helen, his Francophilia seems to be waning, and in recent years he has become deeply involved in viticulture, providing an incredibly useful service by virtue of rubbing the face of the California wine industry in the dirt. Wake up and smell the *terroir,* dudes.

After almost five years of writing about wine, I feel less confident of my grasp of the subject than I did when I began. But I think that on the day I feel confident in my expertise, I'll stop writing about it. Since I have no real training in the official vocabulary of wine tasting—or for that matter, in gardening—you are more likely to find me comparing a wine to a movie, a poem, or a pop song than to an herb or a flower. These are the notes of a passionate amateur, a wordsmith with a wine jones. They are, to borrow a phrase from the late Frederick Exley, *A Fan's Notes.* If you want to learn about malolactic fermentation, I fear your money will be better spent elsewhere.

WHITES, PINKS, GREENS, AND GOLDS

IN THE PINK
ROSÉ

Never have I felt quite so worldly as I did on my very first real date, when, after considered perusal of the wine list, I masterfully commanded the waiter at the Log Cabin restaurant in Lenox, Massachusetts, to fetch me a bottle of Mateus Rosé. In its distinctive Buddha-shaped bottle, with its slight spritz, it represented a step up from the pink Almaden that my friends and I sucked down in order to get into the proper Dionysian frame of mind for the summer rock concerts at Tanglewood. (And that seemed a classic accompaniment—rather like Chablis and oysters—to the cheap Mexican pot we were smoking at the time.) Later, of course, as I discovered the joys of dry reds and whites, I learned to sneer at pink wine; it seemed—as Winston Churchill once remarked regarding the moniker of an acquaintance named Bossom—that it was neither one thing nor the other. A few summers ago a bottle of Domaines Ott rosé in conjunction with a leg of marinated grilled lamb cured me of this particular prejudice; I thought I'd died and gone to Provence, though in fact I was at my friend Steve's birthday party in the Hamptons.

Rosé denotes neither a region nor a grape but a color; it is wine made from almost any variety of red grapes from which the skins are removed after brief flirtation with the clear, fermenting juice. The shade of the wine is a function of the length of contact between skins and juice. (Rosé champagne, confusingly enough, is made with the addition of still red wine to a sparkling white-wine base.) At one time some of the "red" wines of Burgundy were actually pink, prized for their delicate *oeil-de-perdrix* (partridge's eye) color. The color of a rosé wine varies from faint copper to raspberry. And the color of these wines is half their charm. Emile Peynaud, in his classic *The Taste of Wine,* identifies such rosé hues as gray, peony rose, cherry rose, raspberry rose, carmine rose, russet, apricot, onion skin, orange hued, and salmon. Appreciation of such a palette requires the brilliant sunlight of a summer day.

Some years ago, on a stifling July afternoon in Tennessee, my wife and I hosted a garden party to celebrate the christening of our twins. Refusing to settle for beer and Bloody Marys, I decided to offer my guests their choice of Perrier-Jouët champagne or Domaine Tempier rosé. The Tempier was really the perfect choice for the weather and the food—grilled chicken, vegetables, and lamb. Yet I noticed that nobody was drinking the rosé; moreover, I was getting some strange, pitying looks, which at first I attributed to the fact that I had inelegantly sweated right through my linen suit. Finally, standing at the bar, I heard the bartender offer a guest her choice of champagne or white zinfandel. Stifling my first impulse, which was to cuff him sharply about the face and neck, I took the man aside and offered a few trenchant observations, as follows: So-called white zinfandel, with its pinkish or copper tint, is technically a rosé, but generally speaking these California blush wines have every reason to be embarrassed, dim and cloying as they are. At least one hundred makers, led by the prodigious Sutter Home, crank out ten million cases of the stuff each year.

The quality may evolve in time, but for now the makers of California's more interesting pink wines tend to use the word *rosé* for wines that are more flush than blush. The bartender, on being apprised of these facts, agreed to start offering rosé to my guests (who remained unimpressed), and I agreed to try not to be a neurotic geek. Rosés, after all, are not supposed to require a lot of fuss.

Anyone who starts analyzing the taste of a rosé in public should be thrown into the pool immediately. Since I am safe in a locked office at this moment, though, let me propose a few guidelines. A good rosé should be drier than Kool-Aid and sweeter than Amstel Light. It should be enlivened by a thin wire of acidity, to zap the taste buds, and it should have a middle core of fruit that is just pronounced enough to suggest the grape varietal (or varietals) from which it was made. Pinot Noir, being delicate to begin with, tends to make delicate rosés. Cabernet, with its astringency, does not. Some pleasingly hearty pink wines are made from the red grapes indigenous to the Rhône and southern France, such as Grenache, Mourvèdre, and Cinsaut. Regardless of the varietal, rosé is best drunk within a couple of years of vintage.

Among rosé's greatest virtues is its cunning ability to complement any number of foods, particularly those that we tend to associate with summer—not only grilled fish but also grilled meat; spicy food such as Mexican and Thai; and fried seafood dishes. Try a bottle of Bandol with a plate of fried calamari and you'll be converted. We all seem to have some primordial memory of a plate of grilled sardines and a bottle of rosé at an outdoor café overlooking the Mediterranean. For an authentic taste of Provence, look for the '99 Domaine Tempier or the Mas de la Dame. Tavel, from the Rhône Valley (try Vidal-Fleury), was a great favorite of A. J. Liebling. Rosé d'Anjou, from the Loire Valley (such as Charles Joguet's Chinon Rosé), can be nearly as delicious as the southerly juice. Hemingway, always reliable on the subject of country wines, was a big fan of Spanish *rosado,* and good ones are still made in Navarra (Julián Chivite, Gran Feudo Rosado) and Rioja. And yes, Virginia, Portugal still makes the spritzy, semisweet Lancers and Mateus, which no doubt our children will soon rediscover and abuse.

Back in the summer of 1973 I probably derived just as much pleasure from that first bottle of Mateus as I have from any number of first-growth clarets since. Maybe more. I had just acquired my driver's license, I was in the company of my first love; the night and, beyond it, the entire summer stretched out ahead of me like a river full of fat, silvery pink-fleshed fish. And that was what the wine tasted like. It tasted like summer.

WHITE HOPE
CALIFORNIA
CHARDONNAY

When my editor told me that I could write about anything I wanted in my first column so long as it was Chardonnay, I thought briefly about killing her. In the years since Chardonnay has become a virtual brand name I've grown sick to death of hearing my waiter say, "We have a nice Chardonnay." The "house" chard in most restaurants usually tastes like some laboratory synthesis of lemon and sugar. If, on the other hand, you order off the top of the list, you may get something that tastes like five pounds of melted butter churned in fresh-cut oak.

Until recently the more expensive California Chardonnays tended to resemble the women of *Playboy* and Beverly Hills: Their homogeneous voluptuosity often had more to do with technology than with nature. Don't get me wrong, I have nothing against blondes with huge silicone-enhanced breasts. And likewise there's undoubtedly a place for big, heavily oaked, in-your-face Chardonnays. But the oenologists who were graduating from the University of California at Davis in the 1970s and fanning out around Napa and Sonoma seemed to have a single palate among them, and to be aiming to create the vinous equivalent of Chesty Morgan, regardless of the raw materials at their disposal. *Throw in tartaric acid and yeast and then filter the shit out of it, dude.*

In the 1980s, despairing of the domestic product and in lieu of investing in the stock market, I would buy the occasional bottle of white Burgundy. It's produced in France and is, in fact, made from the Chardonnay grape, although the label on any given bottle bears the name of the piece of ground that nurtured the grape rather than the grape itself: Meursault, Puligny-Montrachet, Pouilly-Fuissé, and Chablis are all regions. In Burgundy the allegedly key element of wine personality is the *terroir,* which translates into American as "location, location, location," or, alternately, "dirt." And in Burgundy every other half acre, practically, is a different region. This profusion of appellations, not to mention the abundance of proprietors within each appellation—added to the fact that the weather from year to year in Burgundy is less reliable than in the Napa Valley—is what makes Burgundy, white and red, so difficult to get a handle on, and what leads many New World drinkers to stick to domestic product.

What seemed to me to make white Burgundies worth the effort was the fact that they tended to have more character, to be better balanced, more elegant . . . more, how you say in English . . . more Catherine Deneuve. More *Jules and Jim* than *Die Hard;* less top-heavy and more food-friendly than New World wines. On the other hand, it was and is quite possible to spend forty bucks on a bottle that tastes like it has been barrel-fermented with a big clump of *terroir,* or with Pierre's old socks, or possibly his former cat. Yikes! Rather too much character, *mon cher.*

Fortunately, there is a new generation of California winemakers who seem to be taking lessons from Burgundy without slavishly imitating their French cousins. What they have in common is dedication to low vineyard yields, natural yeasts, French oak, little or no added acid, and little or no filtration. But for those of us who don't make wine and don't really understand how the hell it is made, what these California wines have in abundance is character and elegance, along with some of that ripeness and power that California is notorious for.

Leading the new wave is winemaker Helen Turley, who advises half a dozen of the top California makers and bottles one of the best white wines in the world under her Marcassin label; she happily cops to admiring and emulating the white Burgundies of France's renowned Michel Niellon. A recent trip to Sonoma, nearly converted this California skeptic. And a subsequent tasting organized by *House & Garden* and Geraldine Tashjian of the Burgundy Wine Company suggests that California and Burgundy are no longer worlds apart when it comes to their treatment of the Chardonnay grape. Blind-tasting five similarly priced pairs of '92 Burgundies and '93 Chardonnays was instructive: First of all, it was not always a cinch to identify which was which. I was inclined to think, for instance, that Kistler Vine Hill—matched against the Olivier Leflaive Puligny-Montrachet Champs Gains—was the French, given its lighter body, bright acidity, and slightly grassy taste. I was also surprised to find that two out of my three favorite wines in the tasting were from California—an opinion that was pretty general among the seven tasters. Helen Turley's rare '93 Marcassin Hudson Vineyard, like crème brûlée in a glass, was my personal favorite, followed by the '93 Talbott Sleepy Hollow Vineyard, which I found surprisingly elegant and complex, given my memory of earlier Talbotts as unsubtle and oaky.

Further exploration has yielded an increasing number of beautiful California Chardonnays. Landmark's Overlook, sourced from several areas, is always one of the best values in Chardonnay. Hanzell is making a very sleek and subtle Chardonnay from Sonoma—the '97 is well worth seeking out—while much farther south Greg Brewer and Steve Clifton are crafting amazingly Burgundian wines from Santa Barbara grapes. Helen Turley's Marcassin Vineyards Sonoma Coast Chardonnay has been, for me, the new benchmark ever since the first vintage in '96. The '98 and '99 are practically life changing. The rich, lees-y Turley style can be detected in the several Neyers Chardonnays, made by former Turley protégé Ehren Jordan. Among my perennial favorites are the voluptuous Sonoma County Chardonnays of Steve Kistler. On the same exalted level are the Carneros single-vineyard Chardonnays of newcomer Mike Ramey, whose '98s are already legendary.

I'm changing my mind about California. The movies are getting louder and dumber, but the wines seem to be going the other way.

RIESLING
RECONSIDERED

Growing up in Germany's Black Forest region, Eberhardt Müller was not terribly impressed with the wines of his homeland. Training under chef Alain Senderens at L'Archestrate in Paris, Müller developed a Francophile's sense of textbook food and wine marriages that has served him well since taking over the kitchen at Lutèce, André Soltner's classic New York restaurant. But somewhere along the way he rediscovered German Riesling.

Most Americans tend to think of German wine as being sticky sweet and indifferently vinified. And indeed, an ocean of imported liebfraumilch has confirmed the impression. Blue Nun, anyone? But German wine-making has improved dramatically in the past decade, as has American distribution, and the current fashion for dry white wine has been duly noted. Meantime, Americans are just starting to notice how badly Chardonnay sometimes behaves with food—rather like an obstreperously drunken guest who shouts down the rest of the table. If Chardonnay is the king of white grapes, it can be a tyrant. Riesling, by contrast, is a noble and accommodating queen. And nowhere is Riesling's quicksilver character so variously expressed as on the steep, terraced river valleys of Germany's wine country. Müller recently invited a group of top German winemakers to show their stuff at Lutèce, that shrine of haute French cuisine. More than one skeptic was staggered by the quality of the wines, which ranged from light, super-dry, aperitif-style Rieslings to aged *Trockenbeerenauslesen* with the texture and sweetness of honey. "I don't think there is a grape variety in the world," says Müller, "that produces so many different styles of wine." Indeed, Riesling is a Laurence Olivier of a grape, capable of playing everything from farce to Othello. But for the moment—high summer—it makes sense to focus on the young dry and medium-dry wines that would feel right at home in a picnic basket.

Even when they have residual sugar, German Rieslings have an acidity—partly inherent in the grape and partly a function of cool weather—that counteracts the perception of sweetness. (Think of lemonade: It takes a lot of sugar to tame a handful of lemons.) The high acidity and relatively low alcohol are what make them so refreshing as an aperitif and so food-friendly. Müller proposes this experiment: Grill a piece of fish; try it plain, then dribble some lemon juice on it. The lemon inevitably enhances and highlights the flavor of the fish. And the same is true with wine. The high-acid Riesling makes a much better accompaniment to most fish dishes than the riper (and often heavily oaked) Chardonnay and has the edge to cut through pork dishes and cream sauces. One of the most amazing food-wine combinations I have tasted was Müller's signature oysters with caviar-and-cream sauce, paired with a flinty Mosel Riesling *Spätlese* from Dr. Ernst Loosen. If only the terminology on the label went down as easily as the wine.

Unfortunately, German wine labels make Burgundy look easy. In addition to listing the region, the village, the vineyard, the producer, and the grape, German labels almost always carry a designation indicating the level of ripeness at which the grapes were harvested. Often the same vineyard is harvested several times, the early-harvested grapes providing insurance against bad weather, while the later crop provides a richer, riper wine.

In ascending order of ripeness, the dryish, export-quality wines are *Qualitätswein, Kabinett, Spätlese,* and *Auslese. Qualitätswein* grapes require the addition of sugar to balance their ferocious acidity; from the best makers they produce dry and racy aperitifs, which is also true of the riper *Kabinett,* to which no sugar is added. *Auslese* is nearly a dessert wine, while the slightly less ripe *Spätlese* is perhaps the golden mean of

German Rieslings. However, *Spätlese* can be either dry or semidry—or even semisweet—depending on whether the winemaker decides to stop fermentation before all the sugar has converted into alcohol. Sometimes the label will tell you the style: The word *trocken* on a label indicates the wine is dry; *halbtrocken* is half dry with a touch of residual sugar. (Which won't necessarily make it seem sweeter than the average Napa Chardonnay.) Sometimes the label is silent on this issue; you can get a clue by looking at the alcohol level. A low alcohol level of 8 or 9 percent indicates residual sugar; 10.5 or 11 means the wine is dry, the sugar turned to alcohol.

Five regions account for the best Rieslings: the Mosel-Saar-Ruwer, Nahe, Rheingau, Rheinhessen, and the Pfalz. Each has its own character: The wines of the Mosel region often have a stony element, while those of the Pfalz and Rheingau tend to be a little fatter and fruitier. Across the board, however, they tend to show some combination of tart green apple, lemon, and grapefruit flavors in the drier wines, and pineapple and apricot in the riper ones. While vintages are widely variable in this most northerly of great wine-producing nations, recent vintages, from '93 to the currently available '99, have been good to excellent. Ultimately, it is the producer that counts for quality. Among my favorites, in no particular order, are Geltz Zilliker, Adolph Wingart; George Breuer, Tom Jost; Maximin Grünhauser; Lingenfelder; Dr. Loosen; J. u H. A. Strub; and Schlossgut Diel.

One way to circumvent the almost absurd specificity of German wine labels is to look for the importers' labels: In this country, Terry Theise and Rudolf Weist represent many of Germany's best estates. Their own labels appear separately on the tall, thin bottles that seem to mimic the svelte, racy charms of a good German Riesling.

THE CULT OF CONDRIEU

A few weeks ago a friend called to ask me for the name of a wine I'd selected for the table one night at the Union Square Cafe. He had a serious date coming up and seemed to believe that the wine in question would advance his cause. "It was that one that smelled like the gardens of the Hôtel du Cap," he ventured. The dinner at issue had occurred sometime in the 1980s—a decade whose evenings are not always etched as precisely in memory as one might wish—but I knew exactly what he was looking for.

"Condrieu," I said.

"I think it starts with a *V*," he demurred.

"Viognier is the grape. Condrieu's the region."

He repeated the words several times, rolling the vowels on his tongue as if he found them pleasingly onomatopoeic, and pronounced himself satisfied.

I have had this conversation more than once. Anyone who has ever tasted a good bottle of Condrieu tends to remember the experience—which lingers like the song of Keats's nightingale—if not the name. And I've noticed they are often desperate to remember it before an important amorous engagement. Poking your nose in a glass of Condrieu, you might imagine that you've been dropped into the Garden of Eden, or Kubla Khan's Xanadu as described by the opiated Coleridge. You get the feeling that if orchids had a scent, this might be it. Serena Sutcliffe, Sotheby's statuesque wine muse, told me recently that Condrieu typically evokes May blossoms, but for those of us who haven't been to Sussex recently, this may not ring bells. So let's just say that peaches and apricots form part of the nasal impression and then go straight to the visual analogies: Drinking Condrieu can be like stepping inside a painting by the Tahitian-period Gauguin. At the more ethereal end of the Condrieu spectrum, Fragonard is the artist who comes to mind.

The bad news: Condrieu is about as rare as Han dynasty porcelain and as fragile as Meissen. It's a child star of a wine that tends to turn ugly three or four years after the vintage, just when most great wines are starting to blossom. Prices hover around forty dollars a bottle, which is, to put the best light on it, about what you'd pay for a good Meursault, and a bargain given

Condrieu's scarcity. Perfume is much more expensive, and it's not potable. And Condrieu is much cheaper than visiting the Hôtel du Cap.

Condrieu is made from the fruit of the shy-bearing Viognier vine, grown on the steep, granitic, terraced slopes of the northern Rhône Valley. Only about two hundred acres of vines are currently planted in the entire appellation; an additional six acres of Viognier are planted on the south-facing slopes of the famous Château-Grillet, which is, oddly enough, an appellation unto itself. Marcel Guigal, the king of the northern Rhône, makes one of the best widely available Condrieus. Other fine makers include Georges Vernay, André Perret, Pierre Dumazet, and Jean-Yves Multier's Château du Rozay. Yves Cuilleron produces several great Condrieus, including one of the most exotic white wines in the world: His Condrieu Les Eguets Vendange Tardive is a wildly romantic mouthful of apricot and honey, a wine so rich and sweet as to bear comparison with Château d'Yquem. Les Eguets harks back to the sweeter Condrieu style of the previous century. If you ever score some, save it for the end of the meal. Château-Grillet, the most famous Viognier wine, has had a mixed record. When it's good, as it was in '93, it's very, very good, if not quite as fruity as young Condrieu. Grillet is aged for up to eighteen months in oak, which theoretically gives it great structure and longevity. Certainly it's the only Viognier capable of improving with age. On the other hand, I recently had a ridiculously expensive bottle of the '91 that was completely beat. I'd skip Grillet at present in favor of Condrieu from the '98 and '99 vintages.

Until recently the northern Rhône Valley was the only place Viognier was cultivated. But the cult of Condrieu has lately inspired communicants in other parts of France, and in California, to plant the grape and pray. The results are mixed, but vaguely encouraging. At its best, California Viognier is more Mary Cassatt than Gauguin. So far it seems to be performing better in the New World than Gewürztraminer, which it somewhat resembles, particularly when it's indifferently made. Viognier should be lighter and more ethereal than Gewürztraminer. Napa Valley's Joseph Phelps has had the most experience and the best results outside the Rhône so far with the quirky Viognier grape. His Viognier Vin du Mistal seldom demonstrates the exotic and haunting bouquet of the greatest Condrieu, but it delivers more of the musky Viognier flavor and silky texture than any French examples I've tasted from outside the Rhône Valley. This is no small accomplishment, as you can see by sampling other New World Viogniers. A La Jota I tried recently tasted like root beer.

When you get a taste of a good one, you'll know it. It should be a little like your first encounter with Keats. You will almost certainly suffer some disappointments in your quest. Before tasting, you might help prepare your palate by trying out the word on your tongue: *Viognier, Viognier, Viognier.* Repeat the incantation until ready, then slowly raise the glass . . .

GRÜNER VELTLINER LOVES VEGETABLES

I think one of the reasons I have never been seriously tempted by the vegetarian option is that, in my experience, most wines seem to become surly and depressed when they are forced to associate exclusively with legumes, grains, and chlorophyll-based life-forms. Like girls and boys locked away in same-sex prep schools, most wines yearn for a bit of flesh. But I have recently discovered Grüner Veltliner, an Austrian varietal, which seems to be remarkably friendly with broccoli, tubers, and arugula.

"It's possibly the ultimate vegetarian wine," says Terry Theise, a highly respected Maryland-based importer. Sipping a 1995 Bründlmayer as an accompaniment to a plate of polenta custard with root vegetables at New York's Arcadia restaurant, he says, "There's a certain synergy the palate notices." If Grüner Veltliner, like most Teutonic wines, is a mystery to most Americans, it's not for lack of passion and proselytizing on the part of Theise, who flies around the country saying incredibly mean, witty things about Chardonnay.

While Austria produces beautiful Rieslings, which are generally fatter and riper than their German counterparts, Grüner Veltliner is the most widely planted varietal and perhaps the most intriguing. To me it tastes a little like a theoretical blend of Viognier and Sauvignon Blanc—or, more specifically, of Condrieu and Pouilly-Fumé—combining the wildflower element of the former and the stony, minerally elements of the latter. It sometimes has a kind of wild, peppery element found in neither of these wines, and many tasters note green vegetable elements, which helps explain its compatibility with such foods as green beans and snap peas. It's higher in acid than, say, Pinot Grigio, but like other Austrian whites, it's lower in acid and higher in alcohol than most German Rieslings. It's also almost always a dry wine.

Besides being chlorophyll-friendly, Grüner Veltliner harmonizes beautifully with one other food group: crustaceans. The first time I ever tasted the wine, it was paired with chef Anne Rosenzweig's chimney-smoked lobster at Arcadia. I was thinking Puligny-Montrachet when Rosenzweig emerged from the kitchen in her whites and recommended a '94 Knoll Grüner Veltliner as a perfect match for the dish. I'd never even heard of the stuff, but when a chef of Rosenzweig's abilities gives you a tip, you take it. Exotically lovely as the wine was on first sip, it was even better with the lobster, and I have since discovered that Grüner Veltliner works wonders with shrimp and crab dishes, though I can't really tell you why.

The best Grüners seem to come from the Wachau, Kremstal, and Kamptal regions, in the vicinity of the Danube near the Czech border. While Austrian wine is even less familiar to American drinkers than German wine, it is probably easier for the American ripeness-is-all palate to appreciate. Terry Theise suggests that, in many ways, Austrian wines have more in common with those of Alsace and the Loire than with those of Germany. Until recently, however, the few Austrian wines that made it to this country were seen as cheap alternatives to German wines—"German wannabes," as Theise says. The best wines stayed in Austria. In 1985 a scandal involving certain makers who added diethylene glycol (that is, antifreeze) to their wines severely damaged what little credibility Austrian wines enjoyed abroad, though it resulted in strict new laws and a certain amount of soul searching, which have ultimately been beneficial. "At this point," says Theise, "I think it's one of the most superb and sophisticated wine cultures in the world."

Austria's wine terminology can be nearly as confusing as Germany's, so the best thing to do is ignore most of it. One term that is helpful to know is *Alte Reben*, which means "old vines." Many of the best

Grüners are from older, low-yielding vines. Sometimes the German terms *Spätlese* and *Auslese* are used in addition to specific local terms, but since most Grüners are vinified dry, you can ignore these confusing terms and look at alcohol content. Any wine over 12.5 percent, by law, has had no sugar added, and is therefore naturally ripe. Generally speaking, the higher the alcohol, the richer and more full bodied the Grüner. As is true in most parts of the world, the most important thing to look for is the maker; my favorites include Bründlmayer, Knoll, Nigl, Hirtzberger, and Pichler.

I'm still not quite ready to give up red meat, let alone seafood, but if I ever do, at least I know what to drink alongside my kasha-and-broccoli casserole. In the meantime I have a new excuse to look forward to lobster season.

THE SAVAGE WHITES OF THE LOIRE

Since I first contracted oenophilia I have read—with little comprehension—about the influence on wine of rootstocks, clones, and soil composition, but hardly anything about the importance of onomatopoeia. As a former poet, I can't help suspecting that names may be just as important as soil drainage. The soft consonants and rich, sinuously elided vowels of *Viognier* are, to me, suggestive of that grape's weirdly seductive pleasures. Grape names sometimes reflect perceived taste qualities—as in the case of the eccentric Gewürztraminer, *gewürz* meaning "spice" in German. And Côte-Rôtie (made mostly from Syrah) is so named for its sun-roasted hillside—*roasted* being a word that turns up fairly often in the notes of Côte-Rôtie tasters.

I was considering these semiotic mysteries recently over a glass of Sancerre: To me the hissing double *S* sounds conjure the citric zing of the wine on the tongue, whereas its neighbor across the Loire, Pouilly-Fumé, is often a little rounder and deeper, like its vowels and consonants. Some tasters detect an inherent smoky quality in the latter—*fumé* meaning "smoked" (*Pouilly* is the name of the town). However, in the newly revised *Wine Atlas of France,* Hubrecht Duijker says the Fumé is "so-called because of the smoky film that sometimes covers the berries, not because of any smokiness in the taste."

Actually, it's not easy to tell those two Loire Valley wines apart. Both are made from the Sauvignon Blanc grape—and speaking of names, let's not forget that *sauvignon* derives from *sauvage,* no doubt in honor of this grape's sometimes slashing acidity. California is finally starting to get a grip on this varietal (I like Selene, Rochioli, and Duckhorn). Robert Mondavi was a pioneer, calling his Pouillyesque version Fumé Blanc. New Zealand is becoming a prime source of Sauvignon Blanc; check out the '99 Cloudy Bay. But with the possible exception of the Graves region of Bordeaux, Sauvignon Blanc finds its highest expression in the upper Loire Valley. And after a string of mediocre vintages, the Loire scored back-to-back successes in '95 and '96. If not quite as glorious, the '97, '98, and '99 vintages are all above average.

The acidity of these wines makes for great summer drinking. (Think lemonade.) The word *fresh* inevitably

comes to mind, as in fruit, but also as in the exclamation of the spunky movie heroine in the polka-
dotted dress just before she slaps the guy in the
sharkskin suit. After a swallow of cold Sancerre on a
hot day, you are apt to shake your head vigorously and
blurt something to the effect of "Whew! I needed
that." Almost anyone who aspires to sophistication
claims to like dry wine; Sancerre and Pouilly-Fumé will
put the claim to the test; up against these wines, the average American Chardonnay tastes like Sauternes.

Wherever it's grown, Sauvignon Blanc has a green
vegetable element and often evokes the smell of newly
mown grass. Before we go on, it has to be said that
Sancerre, in particular, sometimes has flavors and aromas that are unmistakably reminiscent of the cat box,
or as the French say, *pipi du chat*. Some lovers of this
grape, like Jacqueline Friedrich, author of the excellent
Wine and Food Guide to the Loire, speak almost fondly
of this quality. (Think white truffles, which also evoke
the sewer.) Importer Neal Rosenthal, who spends quite
a bit of time in the region, believes this aroma is a flaw,
one that he associates with overproduction in the vineyard. "You can't convince me," he says, "that wine is
supposed to smell like that." In riper years, the typical
grapefruit flavors can be replaced with suggestions
of melon, apricot, and peach. The better wines of
Sancerre and Pouilly have a minerally, limestone quality
not unlike that of Chablis; in fact, many of the best
wines of Sancerrois come from outcroppings of the
same Kimmeridgean limestone that predominates in

Chablis. (Pouilly-Fumé is said to show the same "gun-flint" scents, perhaps reflecting the silex—aka flint—in the soil. You may recall the smell if you ever tried to make arrowheads.) Like Chablis, Sancerre and Pouilly-Fumé are great with oysters and other shellfish. One of the greatest Sancerre food matches is with goat cheese, like the region's famed Crottin de Chavignol, although any old chèvre should work.

In the Loire, as elsewhere, the most important thing on the label is the name of the maker. A lot of insipid wine is churned out by the large *négotiants*. Among the most fastidious producers is Pouilly-Fumé's Didier Dagueneau, who is raising the standards in this region even as he infuriates his neighbors with his denunciations of their higher yields and their winemaking techniques. His Silex and Pur Sang bottlings are stunning—and correspondingly expensive. In Sancerre, Lucien Crochet seems equally scrupulous and inspired. Henri Bourgeois in Sancerre and Ladoucette in Pouilly are probably the best large-scale producers; Cotat Frères (Sancerre) and Régis Minet (Pouilly) are two of my favorite small ones.

I should mention that Pouilly-Fumé bears no relation to Pouilly-Fuissé, the latter being a Burgundian Chardonnay. Much as I like a good Chardonnay, summer's the time for a vacation.

HEARTS OF STONE
CHABLIS

Sitting at the tiny front bar at Lutèce the other night, impatiently waiting for a table, I overheard a woman of a certain age ask the bartender for a glass of Chablis. Donning my inquiring journalist hat, I said, "Excuse me, Madam, but by 'Chablis,' do I understand you to mean specifically the flinty, dry white wine produced in the Appellation Contrôlée Chablis region of northern Burgundy, near Auxerre? Or just white wine?" She fled without comment to another part of the restaurant, and later sent her red-faced husband in his bird's-eye Huntsman suit to glare at me. Apparently the great white wines of Chablis are still trying to live down the image problem inflicted on them by the American purveyors of jug wines, and their Australian counterparts, who sold millions of gallons of inexpensive semisweet juice under that name.

Cheap imitators are just the latest in a string of disasters that have dogged this northern outpost of Burgundian viticulture, from nineteenth-century epidemics of mildew and phylloxera to the devastations of both world wars. The soil is thin and tends to wash down the hills. Since Roman times, Chablisians have wrestled with the climate, which is near the edge of the climatic range of grape-growing viability. Frost can strike in the late spring, wiping out the blossoms. It's a wine-making axiom that stress is good for grapes— more or less on the What-Doesn't-Kill-You-Makes-You-Stronger principle—and since the vines of Chablis are, like, *totally* stressed out half the time just trying to survive, the region's wines tend to have the stoic grace and rangy strength of will that we sometimes find in the children of severely dysfunctional marriages.

Though it is made from Chardonnay grapes, Chablis at its most characteristic bears little resemblance to the lush, buttery, buxom style of Chardonnay from warm-weather regions like California and Australia, and is noticeably more austere than the great white Burgundies of the Côte d'Or some eighty miles to the south. If Corton-Charlemagne resembles a novel by one of the Brontë sisters, then Chablis is an early Raymond Carver story. Trying to describe the unique precision of Chablis, tasters often seem to come up with visual analogies like "clean" and "bright." With its stony, crisp quality, it sometimes seems to bear more family resemblance to wines made from Sauvignon Blanc, like Sancerre. "In Chablis," says Al Hotchkin Jr. of the Burgundy Wine Company in New York, "Chardonnay produces a very distinct flavor that's crisp and dry with unique mineral flavor." (Say, "Ah yes, that distinctive *goût de pierre à fusil*" if you wish to impress dining companions.)

Chablis sits on a formation of limestone known as Kimmeridgean, found as far north as Dorset. Many of the best vineyards tend to be thickly strewn with golf-ball-sized pieces of limestone. And you'd swear you can taste those stones in the glass. Which is, perhaps, why Chablis makes such an incredible accompaniment to oysters. The Kimmeridgean is composed in large part of the fossilized shells of Jurassic period oysters (and other bivalves), so it seems natural that there be an affinity. The bright acidity of a young Chablis cuts right to the creamy, briny heart of a Malpeque or a Kumamoto. A little squeeze of lemon may actually enhance the match, but lay off the hot sauce.

Bad to mediocre Chablis has always been more abundant than the good stuff. As in the rest of Burgundy, the producer and the terrain are all-important. Two names to keep in mind: Raveneau and Dauvissat. The Pope and the Dryden of Chablis—now that I think about it, Chablis is definitely a neoclassical wine—Jean-Marie Raveneau and René & Vincent Dauvissat own some of the finest Grand Cru and Premier Cru vineyards. Both domains use a small percentage of new-oak barrels, but not so many as to mask the distinctive flinty heart of the appellation. Their wines, particularly Grand Crus like the magnificent Les Clos, are at their best after eight to ten years of aging. Although they are not exactly cheap—always north of thirty dollars—they are an excellent value compared to the Grand Crus from the Côte d'Or, which often start at a hundred dollars.

Challenging the R and D supremacy is the *négotiant* Verget, run by the eccentric Jean-Marie Guffens, who uses more new oak, and whose Montée de Tonnerre is a spicier, slightly less characteristic wine. Best known to Americans for their generic Moreau Blanc and Rouge, J. Moreau et Fils uses no wood whatsoever in their various Chablis, which tend to be among the cleanest—some would say leanest—and the most lemony.

You stand an excellent chance of getting a fine bottle if you buy any of the hillside-grown Grand Crus—the highest appellation—or Premier Crus, particularly in the recent vintages of '95, '96, '97, and '99. Joseph Drouhin, Louis Michel, and Jean Dauvissat (related to René and Vincent) are names to look for. Farther down the classification scale, the best makers, such as Michel Barat, produce elegant wines under the uninflected "Chablis" label. These wines typically sell for well under twenty dollars. "Petit Chablis," the lowest classification, is best avoided, unless you're making salad dressing and there's no balsamic vinegar in the house.

NUMBER TWO
AND TRYING
HARDER
CALIFORNIA
SAUVIGNON BLANC

If Chardonnay is the Coke of the white-wine universe, then Sauvignon Blanc ranks somewhere between Pepsi and RC Cola. In the fertile vineyards of California, even at riotously high yield levels, Chardonnay achieves a voluptuous ripeness that speaks to the secret sweet tooth in all of us. Sauvignon Blanc, on the other hand, has to be severely disciplined in the climatic Eden of California or else it can taste lean, weedy, and rank. Until recently, New World vintners were still trying to figure out how to tame this feral child of a grape. Finally, many have begun to succeed. It's now quite possible to find a California Sauvignon Blanc that is less expensive, more refreshing, and more food-friendly than that other white wine.

Although it probably originated in Bordeaux, where it is still the prime ingredient in that region's whites, the Sauvignon Blanc grape is most closely associated with the upper Loire Valley, and in particular with the wines of Sancerre and Pouilly-Fumé. At their best, these wines are bone-dry, with a spine of citrusy acidity. In a good, warm year the fruit is reminiscent of grapefruit, melon, peaches, even figs. At one end of the stylistic spectrum Sancerre and Pouilly-Fumé exhibit a grassy, herbal taste; at the other end, a flinty mineral quality. The seductive appeal of a good Loire Sauvignon Blanc is more reminiscent of the gamine than of the odalisque. At its least attractive it is reminiscent of cabbage and the cat box.

Not surprisingly, the California versions of Sauvignon Blanc are stylistically all over the map, although in recent years, thank God, I have encountered far fewer that evoke what the French call *pipi du chat*. They are never as fat and buttery as the richest California Chardonnays, although some makers use oak barrels and malolactic fermentation to create a Chardonnay-like style and to tame the sometimes fierce acidity. Robert Mondavi was the first to go in this direction. Moreover, in a bit of Madison Avenue sleight of hand, to invest the then unpopular grape with a bit of glamour, he called his wine Fumé Blanc, in honor of Pouilly-Fumé. Although it's not a hard-and-fast rule, the winemakers who have followed his nomenclature seem to emulate this bigger, smoother style. The other extreme is a light, citrusy, zippy beverage that smells like a new-mown field—grass with a smattering of dandelions. Between these two poles you should be able to find a California SB to suit your taste.

For some reason, several of the best California Sauvignon makers also specialize in Merlot, another French-speaking grape that wasn't easily translated into Napa and Sonoma Valleyspeak. (Like SB, Merlot can get weedy and vegetal in warmer climates, particularly when it's overcropped.) Mia Klein, a diminutive and intensely enthusiastic native of Hermosa Beach, makes one of the very best California Merlots under her Selene Wines label. She is also a sorceress with Sauvignon Blanc—the Didier Dagueneau of California. "Both varietals had a lot of room for improvement when I started out," she says. "They were considered secondary varietals." Since her first vintage, in 1992, Klein has helped change that perception. Her '97 Selene Hyde Vineyard Sauvignon Blanc, from the cool Carneros region, is a full-color catalog of the most attractive flavors of the grape, combining a ripe melony character with the treble notes of Key lime and wheatgrass.

Matanzas Creek, another winery renowned for its Merlots, also makes a complex SB that costs about one-fifth of what it gets for its Journey Chardonnay. And Duckhorn, which did as much as any winery to popularize Merlot in this country, makes a beautiful example in quantities sufficient to turn up at your local Liquor Locker. Harder to find, but worth the trouble, is the Sauvignon Blanc from Rochioli, the Pinot Noir boutique in the Russian River Valley. And their neighbors at Martinelli, one of my favorite wineries, make one that's so rich it could easily be mistaken for a Chardonnay, which may or may not be a good thing.

Because it is usually higher in acid than Chardonnay (or Sémillon, with which it is blended in Bordeaux), Sauvignon Blanc accompanies a far greater range of food. Almost any kind of fish does well with SB—which provides roughly the same flavor-enhancing service as lemon juice. (Not to keep bashing away at good old Chardonnay, but it can obliterate delicate white fish.) To me, a good Sauvignon Blanc should conjure up a picnic in a meadow, with scruffy wildflowers sprinkled amid the grasses and the faintest funky scent of a distant farm on the breeze. Kissing would definitely be part of these bucolic festivities, a little light petting perhaps, but nothing heavier than that. Hey—it's not that kind of wine, if you know what I mean.

CHAMPAGNE
AND BUBBLY

BEAUTIFUL
BUBBLEHEADS

Upon first tasting the sparkling wine of Champagne, Dom Pérignon is said to have called out to a fellow friar: "Come quickly, I'm tasting stars." Apocryphal or not, this is surely one of the best descriptions in the history of wine commentary.

As the new year, *voilà!*, approaches, it behooves us to renew our acquaintance with this most accessible of luxuries. First of all, let's be clear about this, champagne comes from France. If you're the kind of guy who buys his fiancée a cubic zirconia on the principle that it looks just like the real thing, then by all means celebrate your nuptials with Spanish bubbly. Second: There *is* such a thing as bad French champagne, which you may dimly remember from your last trip to that strip joint on the Place Pigalle, but so far as I can tell, almost none of it is exported to the States.

The cool, pale beauty of champagne is, like that of Ingrid Bergman and Greta Garbo, the product of a chilly climate. The cold Champagne winters tended to interrupt the fermentation process before it was complete; in the spring, after the wine had been bottled, the warm weather brought on a second fermentation of the remaining sugars, creating carbon dioxide. Once considered a nuisance, the bubbles eventually became a trademark. Vintage-dated champagne is created only in those exceptional years when the grapes achieve optimum ripeness before the onset of cold weather. Nonvintage champagne is a blend of juice from less ripe years with reserve stocks from previous years and from diverse vineyards; the master winemakers of Champagne seek a whole that is greater than the parts. In champagne, two plus two often equals five, or even seven.

For many imbibers, the difference between, say, the NV Veuve Clicquot (about forty dollars) and the vintage-dated '95 (about sixty dollars) may illustrate the law of diminishing returns. On the other hand, champagne is not made for economists. Vintage champagne tends to have more complexity and finesse than the generic bubbly. Most houses are currently offering the excellent '95 vintage, which looks to be more successful than '93, the latest generally declared vintage. Watch for the excellent '96s, to be released in 2001. One step up from mere vintage champagne are the so-called *têtes du cuvées,* the super-luxury bottlings that come from the best Grand Cru vineyards and tend to arrive at the liquor store in very fancy-looking bottles. Among the best known and most widely available of these are Dom Pérignon, Cristal, Veuve Clicquot Grande Dame, and Perrier-Jouët Fleurs de Champagne. The house of Krug only makes *têtes du cuvée*—including the multivintage Grand Cuvée and the single-vineyard, all-Chardonnay Clos du Mesnil. If you can still find any, look for these grand marques in the celestial '90 vintage, one of the best of the century. Dom Pérignon made a lighter-than-usual '92, while Cristal and other houses put out a '93. My advice, if you have the choice, is to skip from '90 to '95.

Which leads to the question: Is beluga four times as good as sevruga? Is Dom Pérignon worth four bottles of Moët & Chandon? If you are a connoisseur, a lover, a snob, or the owner of a large oceangoing craft, the answer to the last question is probably yes.

Champagne is famously versatile, but each one has its perfect occasions. To illustrate this we might propose a book of hours—a theoretical day of champagne. During the daylight hours, we would want a light, crisp, and refreshing champagne. Perrier-Jouët is made in this style, and is remarkably affordable. I can't think of a more elegant luncheon beverage than a rosé champagne like Billecart-Salmon (tinted with the addition of a small amount of still, red wine). As an aperitif, to start the evening in style, it's hard to beat a *blanc de blanc* such as Drappier, which is made exclusively from white Chardonnay grapes; it's usually lighter and sprightlier than traditional champagne. Once the appetizers come out, you would naturally open one of the bolder nonvintage blends, like a Bollinger or a Veuve, which are dominated by the black-skinned Pinot Noir and Pinot Meunier grapes. For a main course involving fish or fowl, one would crave the subtle complexities of a vintage champagne like Pol Roger's '95. If you are faced with heavier fare, you would want the huge, winy, autumnal Krug Grande Cuvée. And finally, with dessert, the semisweet Moët & Chandon Demi Sec.

This hypothetical schedule inevitably leads us to the question of the champagne hangover—a powerful myth that seems to derive in part from vague memories of weddings and other fêtes when the champers was poured liberally on top of cocktails and red wine and often seasoned with clouds of tobacco and cannabis. A recent, highly unscientific experiment with three subjects and five bottles of champagne consumed with food—sushi, in fact—over the course of several hours suggests that if you don't mix, you shouldn't worry. But neither should you necessarily appear on the Charlie Rose show the next day.

Finally, a word about glasses: the phallic flute is the only way to go. The shallow parfait dish so often seen at badly catered weddings diffuses the nose and the bubbles, although it has the possible aesthetic virtue of deriving, originally, from a mold of Marie Antoinette's breast.

IF YOU HAVE
TO ASK...
TÉTES DE CUVÉES
CHAMPAGNE

Let's start with some basic definitions: Wine, as Thomas Jefferson noted, is a necessity. Champagne is usually presumed to be a luxury, although a good case could be made for its necessity; without it, weddings, New Year's Eve, and champagne brunches are inconceivable. Dom Pérignon, however, is definitely a luxury. Ditto Cristal, Krug, and Veuve Clicquot's La Grande Dame.

Luxury cuvée champagne is a special category that represents 13 percent of the American champagne market; it often comes in unusually shaped, sometimes overwrought bottles that sell for a hundred bucks and up. It's almost always from a great vintage year (although Krug's Grande Cuvée is multivintage). These prestige cuvées are basically couture versions of the major champagne domains' ready-to-wear bottling (although some houses, like Salon and Krug, are devoted exclusively to luxury cuvées). Like couture dresses, they're often accompanied by a string of pearls, *le collier de perles* being the term for the fine ring of delicate bubbles that adorn a glass of very well-made champagne. As for the question of whether Cristal is worth five times (around $150) the nonvintage Roederer (around $30), one can only answer, if you have to ask . . . Is beluga four times as good as sevruga? On the other hand, a $200 bottle of Dom Pérignon Rosé—closer to $400 if you're in a restaurant—could seem incredibly cheap if you are trying to close a deal, of either the commercial or the romantic variety. Which brings us to a tricky point: Many of these wines are purchased and consumed as a statement rather than as a beverage. In such cases the label is more important than the juice. And the label that speaks every language known to the United Nations is named for the seventeenth-century monk who invented modern champagne.

Wine buffs have one thing in common with punk-rock fans: There's a certain presumption of guilt about a band or a wine that becomes too famous. "We think Dom Pérignon can't be good because the stars drink it," wine critic Jancis Robinson told me recently. "But in fact, you will never be disappointed." Like a head banger dissing Nirvana after *Nevermind*, I was one of those reverse snobs about DP. The '88 vintage, which was a little tough for my taste, tended to confirm my skepticism when it was first released. But the sensational

'90 vintage—and a tasting of mature vintages dating back to '75—has made a new believer out of me. Even if they hadn't, meeting head winemaker Richard Geoffroy might have charmed me into a favorable impression.

The fortyish Geoffroy's enthusiasm is such that his hair seems to stand up a little higher as he explains the arduous blending process or the Dom Pérignon house style, which for him has to do with a certain silkiness of texture rather than a consistent set of flavors. Geoffroy comes by his passion honestly, descending from a long line of grape growers in the Champagne region. Somewhere along the way he decided to get his M.D., but before he'd even begun to practice medicine, he returned to school to study oenology and then went to work for the house of Moët & Chandon. He became head winemaker at DP just in time to take charge of the '90 vintage, which is one of the greatest young champagnes I've ever encountered.

Dom Pérignon does not release production figures, but case production certainly reaches into the five-figure range, which makes the quality all the more remarkable. At the other end of the luxury cuvée spectrum, the venerable family-run domain of Krug produces less than a thousand cases of its Clos du Mesnil *blanc de blanc*. While two grape varieties and dozens of barrels will eventually be employed to produce a DP, Clos du Mesnil is made of 100 percent Chardonnay grapes from a single four-acre vineyard, recognized for three hundred years as one of the most favored pieces of ground in Champagne. What to eat with your $250 bottle of

Clos? Almost anything is one answer, but Rémi Krug, who represents the fifth generation of Krugs, thinks that popcorn may be the ideal food match, a proposition he proved for me one afternoon at Manhattan's Osteria del Circo over four bowls of popcorn and three bottles of Krug.

My son, a big popcorn fan, has lately taken to categorizing people in terms of their hair color; whenever a name is mentioned, he asks, "What color hair he have?" As a taxonomic principle for humans it may be arbitrary, but it actually lends itself nicely to the world of luxury cuvée champagnes. Though they are mostly gold in color, prestige cuvées are made out of varying proportions of white and black grapes. *Blanc de blanc* is the term for 100 percent Chardonnay wines, which tend to be more delicate and citrusy than those that have a higher proportion of Pinot Noir. Taittinger Comtes de Champagne *blanc de blanc* and Dom Ruinart *blanc de blanc* are outstanding examples. Dom Pérignon is usually somewhere between blond and brunette, while Cristal's higher proportion of Pinot makes it more of a brunette. Among the most Pinot-heavy of the prestige cuvées are the rare Bollinger Tradition R.D. and Veuve Clicquot's La Grande Dame.

If you want to impress a wine buff, and for that matter your own palate, it may be worth seeking out such lesser-known top-shelf bottlings as Philpponnat's Clos des Goisses, Nicolas Feuillatte Palme d'Or, or Salon *blanc de blanc*. On the other hand, if you want to woo a client, or a date, you can't go wrong with the DP.

EAST MEETS WEST: KAISEKI CUISINE AND VINTAGE FRENCH CHAMPAGNE

Master chef Joël Robuchon, who recently retired from his eponymous three-star Paris restaurant, was skeptical. He had been invited, along with other food and wine buffs, to Château de Saran, an eighteenth-century manor owned by Moët & Chandon, to experience an evening of Dom Pérignon champagne and Japanese kaiseki cuisine. The experiment was the brainchild of Richard Geoffroy, the effervescent *chef de cave* for Dom Pérignon. When he's not in the Moët cellars beneath the town of Épernay, Geoffroy travels the globe as an ambassador for the world's most famous luxury beverage, and his culinary exploration has led him to an obsession with the affinities between champagne and Asian cuisine. He became particularly inter-

ested in kaiseki, the ethereal haute cuisine of aristocratic Kyoto, which ultimately derives from Zen temple
cooking. Last November he convinced Yoshihiro Murata, one of Japan's most accomplished chefs, to come
to Épernay for a week to explore the synchronicity of
kaiseki and bubbly.

According to Geoffroy, Robuchon's skepticism
faded fast: By the third of eleven courses he was furi-
ously scribbling notes, and by the end of the meal he
announced that he had experienced an epiphany.
Having lived in Japan and washed down a fair amount
of champagne with sushi, I was probably less skeptical
when I arrived a few days later. But still, I was unprepared for the revelations that awaited me.

It's hard to imagine two cuisines less alike than
French and Japanese. "French cooking has more in
common with Chinese," says Geoffroy. "Both are about
the fusion of elements and processing. Italian is closer to
Japanese—they are about the purity of ingredients.
Especially in kaiseki." However, Japanese cooking and
champagne have one important ingredient in common.
"It's the yeast," says Geoffroy, presiding over the table
in the dining room at the Château de Saran.

The harvest was completed a few days ago; the hillside vineyards outside have turned to gold. Although
this is the last of a week's worth of such dinners, Geoffroy seems ridiculously excited by the prospect of the
meal ahead—like a matchmaker who believes he's about
to unite two royal families. His perpetually surprised-
looking hair and the irregular line of his front teeth add

to the impression of eager boyishness. "Japanese cooking is based on fermented foods—sake, soy sauce, miso, and daizu. Yeast is the key." And no wine is quite so prominently yeasty as twice-fermented champagne. ("Bread" and "toast" are among the most frequent notes cited by champagne tasters.) Other sparkling wines, including those from California, seldom show their yeasty quality so prominently as those from the cool-weather Champagne region. "In California," says Geoffroy, "the fruit character is so strong that the yeast can't get through the door. For me, champagne is about the marriage of fruit and yeast."

The first marriage of the evening involves matsutake mushrooms and '85 Dom Pérignon. The Portobello-sized matsutakes are the truffles of Japanese cooking. Like the ingredients for this dinner—as well as Murata's staff and all the dinnerware—they have been flown in fresh from Japan. The matsutakes are grilled over charcoal braziers as we watch. More ethereal than truffles, they are served on creamy-glazed earthenware trays with a wedge of sudachi, a tiny Japanese lime. The earthy, smoky taste of the grilled mushroom and the bite of the lime are amazingly similar to the flavors of the '85 DP. Other courses involve more contrapuntal relationships. I'll never forget the fourth-course toro—the most desirable cut of the tuna, from the belly; its fatty richness made the '85 DP seem slim and racy. I can't even begin to describe the relationships involved in the fifth-course "transgressive fusion" dish: a lily-bulb-paste dumpling wrapped around a ball of foie gras and sprinkled with truffles and crushed quail skull. Nice try—but I prefer the traditional kaiseki dishes, like the monkfish liver, and the abalone and uni (sea urchin) cooked in seaweed and salt. I also like the grilled fugu (poison blowfish), which always adds a certain Russian roulette frisson to a good kaiseki dinner. The coup de grâce, however, is a simple bowl of perfectly cooked short-grained sticky rice, topped with beluga caviar. Washed down, of course, with more '85 Dom Pérignon.

It's difficult to find real kaiseki cooking in the States, and most of us can't afford to drink Dom Pérignon very often, but the principles of the Château de Saran dinners are transferable to your local sushiya. Miso, like soy sauce, is very champagne-friendly. And champagne somehow holds its own against all but the largest doses of wasabi, the piquant, pale green horse-radishlike root that generally accompanies sashimi. Vinegar, however, is a wine killer: Those Japanese dishes that rely on it should be accompanied by sake.

"It's about suggesting and opening doors," says Geoffroy of his grand experiment, as he pours '59 Dom Pérignon in the parlor after dinner. Sipping the shockingly youthful beverage, I am thinking that Kipling may have been wrong about East and West. On this particular rainy night in Champagne, the twain have met.

A TICKET TO THE VENETO

When you sit down at a trattoria in Florence or Venice, chances are pretty good that a flute of sparkling wine will be placed in front of you. This will be Prosecco, the light, slightly sweet, slightly fizzy teaser that comes from the steep hills near Conegliano, a walkable-sized town about an hour north of Venice. One theory about Prosecco is that it tastes best in situ and loses its charm the farther it travels from northern Italy. The other theory is that it can stimulate the faculty that method actors call sense memory, allowing us, wherever we may find ourselves, to re-create the illusion of a hedonistic summer afternoon in the Veneto.

Prosecco is not Cristal, nor is it meant to be. Here in the States it goes for about ten bucks a bottle, and at the right alfresco moment it can be immensely refreshing, with its sweetish come-on and its slightly bitter finish—rather like a flirtatious look exchanged across a courtyard that briefly illuminates the scene before the other party turns away forever. I'd never say no to a glass of Krug or Dom Pérignon, but sometimes a bowl of *spaghetti aglio olio* can be more satisfying than châteaubriand. Likewise Prosecco. I think of it as a spring-summer fling.

Mario Batali, the gregarious, Falstaffian proprietor of New York's Pó and Babbo restaurants and a star of the Food Network, is a big Prosecco fan. "It's not nearly as elegant as champagne," he says, "but it's much more drinkable. You can drink it with anything. As an aperitif, it's nonpareil. And it really comes into its own as a mixer, especially with fruit juice." Prosecco is the traditional base of the famous Bellini, invented at Harry's Bar in Venice. At Babbo, Batali serves many variations, including blood orange and green apple Bellinis.

Prosecco is not a regional name but the name of a white-grape variety indigenous to Friuli. Any wine made anywhere from the grape can be called Prosecco, but the best bear the title Prosecco di Conegliano-Valdobbiadene. The steep vineyards of the region beyond Conegliano, dotted with monasteries and castles, are among the most beautiful in the world. Like champagne, the wine made from Prosecco came by its bubbles honestly. The juice from these late-ripening grapes would often cease fermentation during the cold winters, leaving residual sugar. The warm weather of spring would set off a secondary fermentation, releasing CO_2 into the wine. Current production methods mimic this process, creating wine that is either still, *frizzante* (slightly fizzy), or *spumante* (fizzier).

The *frizzante* style seems to best suit this light wine, although the finest Prosecco I've ever had was made in the bubblier *spumante* style by a producer called Varaschin, whose wine I first tasted while participating in a literary festival in Conegliano. It was served at lunch, and when I expressed my admiration for the Prosecco the host of the festival offered to drive me to see the vineyards and taste in the cellar, explaining that it was only fifteen minutes away. Two vertiginous hours later we arrived at our destination, near the town San Pietro di Barbozza. Several generations debouched from a farmhouse, which was perched amid vineyards on a hill. I became fairly fluent in Italian as I tasted through the range of their wines, though I've never really spoken it before or since. As darkness fell, I stopped worrying that I was going to be spectacularly late for my reading that night. Varaschin makes fairly serious, champagnelike Prosecco; as in champagne, the two cuvées are labeled "brut" (dry) and "semidry" (sweet). Much as I liked both, I think Prosecco is best when it's got a touch of sugar, which is the native style. I was clapped heartily on the back when I made this observation and if I'm not mistaken, my intelligence and discrimination were commended by all present.

The general impression of a Prosecco should be clean and fresh and slightly lemony; nevertheless, there is sometimes a hint of brandy. If you get one that tastes too much like brandy, send it back. Yelling at the purveyor in Italian and waving your arms around is not necessary, although it's very authentic. The chief enemy of Prosecco is age; this is a wine to be consumed shortly after it's released, which in the States is usually late spring. Unfortunately, it's hard to tell when it's produced. I've seen only a couple that were vintage-dated, and Proseccos lose their freshness more rapidly than nonvintage champagne, which may be one reason they taste best close to the source. But most of us can't be in Italy all the time, and when we can't, Prosecco is one simple way to get a summertime fix of *sprezzatura*.

SCHRAMSBERG DON'T MAKE ME CRAZY

Branding seems to be the buzzword of the new millennium. Creating a brand name with a marketable image is the goal of almost every new business enterprise. Hence the spectacle of rap stars attaching their names to clothing lines, and clothing designers stamping their brand on bureaus and four-poster beds. In the world of consumer luxury goods, image is more important than substance. Which is part of the challenge facing California's sparkling-wine makers. The name *champagne* is one of the most potent and venerable of all luxury brands—a universal synecdoche for the good life. When was the last time you said to your loved one, "Honey, I want to lick sparkling wine off your naked body?" Or, "Let's break out the Iron Horse"?

Somehow the substitution of the words *champagne* or *Cristal* makes these declarations more plausible.

By *champagne*, of course, we mean the sparkling wine produced in the Champagne region of north-central France. Or do we? Even among northern California's bubbly producers there seems to be some disagreement. Most of them call their product "sparkling wine" and emphasize that champagne is different—that is to say, Gallic apples next to their California oranges, not necessarily better or worse. But comparison is inevitable. Same grapes, same method, same section of the wine store. Eventually the question arises: How good is the California stuff in relation to the original? California's pioneer bubbly makers insist on challenging the French head-on and calling their top wines "Napa Valley Champagne."

In 1965, a year before Robert Mondavi started his eponymous winery, Jack and Jamie Davies bought the old Jacob Schram winery on the eastern slope of Napa Valley's Diamond Mountain and dubbed it Schramsberg. One of Napa's pioneers, Schram arrived in Napa in 1857. Within a couple of decades his wines were winning international acclaim. Robert Louis Stevenson wrote about his 1880 visit in his book *Silverado Squatters*. The acerbic Ambrose Bierce was a frequent visitor before he disappeared in the desert. Prohibition put the winery out of business. The absurdly charming Queen Anne house on the hillside served as a vacation home for a succession of owners until the Davieses arrived, quixotically determined to restore the winery and produce a French-style sparkling wine using the traditional Pinot Noir and Chardonnay grapes.

At that time California sparkling wine was a semi-sweet concoction made by a shortcut method from inferior grapes. There was very little Chardonnay or Pinot Noir planted in the valley. Somehow the Davieses conjured up some local chard. When the press failed to operate for their first crush, petite blond Jamie, formerly an art dealer, took off her shoes and jumped in the press to stomp the grapes with her feet. That vintage was released two years later, the first California vintage-dated sparkling wine made with Chardonnay grapes. In 1972 Schramsberg *blanc de blanc* (literally "white of white," meaning all-Chardonnay) landed on the map when Nixon brought the '69 vintage to Beijing to toast Chinese Premier Chou En-lai. Not that the world necessarily rushed to embrace California bubbly.

I still had my doubts when I visited Napa a few months ago. Schramsberg's winemaker Mike Reynolds and Hugh Davies, the second-generation Davies at the winery, were determined to put a dent in my Francophilia. The boyish, Gen X duo are used to this kind of skepticism. They have a simple response: blind tasting. After a tour of the nineteenth-century cellars, they sat myself and *House & Garden* food editor Lora Zarubin down in front of five mysterious hooded bottles. All we knew for certain was that one of the bottles was Schramsberg's top-of-the-line J Schram. The others were super-premium (*aka têtes du cuvées*) French champagnes, not just your nonvintage bruts but the big boys—the ones that go for a hundred bucks and up. When the bubbles had cleared and the bottles had been unveiled, I discovered I'd rated the '93 J Schram in second place, tied with the '92 Dom Pérignon, ahead of the '95 Perrier-Jouët Fleurs de Champagne and the '90 Pol Roger Winston Churchill. (My unequivocal first pick was the '90 Veuve Clicquot Grande Dame.) Lora, veteran of several trips to Champagne, put the J Schram in first place. Mike picked his own wine second after the Pol Roger, while Hugh, who said he tried to avoid rating the Schram first, did so anyway.

Among the first fans of Schramsberg wines were the folks at the venerable champagne house of Moët & Chandon, who, after inquiring about buying the winery, purchased land for their own Napa Valley sparkling-wine operation in 1973. Mumm, Roederer, Piper Heidsieck, and Taittinger followed Moët to California. While the expertise of these venerable marques accelerated the improvement of California bubbly, their French roots have resulted in a curious identity crisis. "The fact that so much of the development was done by French companies made for confusion about whether these California wines were second labels," says Dawnee Dyer, the talented American winemaker at Chandon. The French companies can hardly be expected to tout the superiority of the California product. Hence the apples-and-oranges line of thinking.

The typical California bubbly tastes fruitier and riper than the typical champagne. Some California makers, like Dyer and Greg Fowler at Mumm, emphasize *le difference,* going for a bold, fruity signature, while others, like Schramsberg's Reynolds, aim for a sleek and elegant champagnelike style. Having been weaned on the products of Reims and Épernay, I tend to prefer the latter, but this is a matter of taste. I'm surprised to admit that after several days of tasting, I've overcome my blanket prejudice against California bubbles. There are plenty of good ones. Dollar for dollar, they are probably a better value than the French stuff. But of course, if markets were strictly about value, I probably wouldn't be wearing these Prada loafers.

REDS

THE DISCREET CHARMS OF VOLNAY

I seem to remember one of Ann Beattie's more jaded characters once dismissing another character by remarking that he couldn't tell the difference between Burgundy and Bordeaux. I remember feeling very small-town when I read that, years ago, knowing that the description fit me. I guess I've come a long way, because I concluded recently that I *could* tell the difference: If it's red, French, costs too much, and tastes like the water that's left in the vase after the flowers have died and rotted, it's probably Burgundy.

Burgundy is to wine what the Balkans are to geopolitics. It's impossible to figure out. You can't get a decent bottle for less than ten dollars, and what's worse, you can pay sixty or seventy bucks for some real rotgut—and I'm talking retail, before the outrageous markup charged by your friendly neighborhood bistro. The only rational conclusion is that it's not worth the effort—until you taste a good one. And then it's hard to forget, although difficult to describe. As Evelyn Waugh wrote of the elusive beverage in *Brideshead Revisited:* "For centuries every language has been strained to define its beauty, and has produced only wild conceits or the stock epithets of the trade."

My first revelation as to the alchemically predestined marriage of the Pinot Noir grape and Côte d'Or weather and soil was an '85 village Volnay—I don't remember the estate. I do remember thinking: *Hey, whoa . . . so this is what the fuss is about.* Volnay has since become a touchstone; I have found it to be uncharacteristically reliable for Burgundy and immensely seductive. Volnay is slightly less renowned now than it was in the Middle Ages, when it was the favorite of Louis XI and the Knights of Malta. The region's lack of officially designated Grand Cru vineyards somewhat reduces its snob appeal, though many experts think some of Volnay's vineyards to be worthy of the distinction. Whether the Volnaysiens were insufficiently politically adroit when the classifications were made, or worried about paying higher taxes on Grand Cru acreage, the happy result for customers is, by Burgundian standards, a less outlandish quality-to-price ratio. More than half the vineyards in Volnay are Premier Cru, the second highest designation, and—as in Bordeaux's Saint-Julien—the overall level of winemaking is very high.

The standard rap on Volnay is that it has more finesse than power—in comparison to, say, the wines of

nearby Pommard. Volnay fans often refer to its ethereal, perfumed quality. Scents of lilac and violet are said
to be found in the glass. In the earthier Burgundies the
nose tends more toward the barnyard, and even to that
great raw material for the flower bed, namely, horse-
shit. Welcome to the strange and wonderful world of
Burgundy, where our aesthetic slides between the poles
of power and finesse, the floral and the excremental.
Auberon Waugh—son of Evelyn—once noted that the
English seem especially to favor the latter aromas in
their Burgundy; if this doesn't sound compatible with
your good old American chicken potpie, you will probably be happy with the relative polish of Volnay.

Generally speaking, Volnay is more Watteau than
Brueghel, more Jaguar than Porsche (just as it's generally true that Bordeaux is more powerful than
Burgundy). But there is an extraordinary range of styles
even within this 527-acre appellation, reflecting different soil types and vinification practices. The wines of
Michel Lafarge, for instance, are extremely big and burly
when compared with the lacy, feminine Volnays of
Marquis d'Angerville. Then there is the busty, fruity
style of Domaine de Comte Lafon, the great Meursault
producer. All these wines make a great accompaniment
to a simple roast chicken or game bird; I think beef and
lamb overwhelm the red berry flavors typical of Volnay.

While Bordeaux was far from blessed in the 1990s,
the Burgundians were luckier. Nineteen ninety was a
spectacular vintage and the wines, especially the Volnays,
are now approaching their peak. Ninety-one has a poor
reputation, although I have had brilliant wines from

Lafarge and Pousse d'Or in this vintage. D'Angerville did well in the so-so '92 vintage. Ninety-three was an excellent year for red wines throughout the Côte d'Or. In June 2000 I had a lavish, silky Bouchard Père et Fils '93 Volnay Premier Clos de Rougets, which was one of the best Volnays I've tasted. Both '95 and '96 were excellent vintages, though the Premier Crus shouldn't be touched before 2001. Meantime, drink the friendly, early-maturing '97s and try like hell to buy as much of the '99 vintage as you can afford. The Burgundians are claiming it's another '90, and having tasted some barrel samples in Beaune this past summer, I'm inclined to agree.

Be advised—cellaring Burgundy is a dicey business. It's much more susceptible to temperature than Bordeaux—keep it below sixty degrees—and the window of maturity is much narrower. Some of the '88s—which I bought and laid down after some forgotten financial windfall because they were supposed to be so long lived—have been crapping out on me, although I recently drank a rich and berry-packed '88 Volnay Pousse d'Or from the venerable Volnay Domaine de la Pousse d'Or, which was just coming online.

A final piece of advice from A. J. Liebling: "Burgundy is a lovely thing when you can get anybody to buy it for you."

ZIN WENT THE STRINGS OF MY HEART

"Blackberry, blackberry, blackberry . . ."
—Robert Hass, "Meditation at Lagunitas"

When I married a southerner some years ago, I started wrestling with the urgent problem of which wine to serve with fried chicken. Red Burgundy and Pinot Noir don't stand up to the oil. Ditto old Bordeaux. Big, tannic Cabernets seem to overwhelm the white meat. Monster Chardonnays sort of work. Bibulous hours of trial and error finally provided the answer: red zinfandel. I have since discovered that zinfandel is the answer to many questions, including, just possibly, what is the Great American Red-Wine Varietal?

The origins of zinfandel are swathed in mystery, but if it's not native, it's been in this country since at least the early nineteenth century. The California gold rush miners swigged it down by the barrelful. Many of us, as younger oenophiles, guzzled it under the name of Gallo Hearty Burgundy. More recently the big wineries concocted a beverage called *white* zinfandel—actually sort of a coppery pink—mass-produced on overcropped land from grapes whose black skins have been removed. On that subject, 'nuff said.

Attending the Zinfandel Advocates and Producers (ZAP) tasting in San Francisco is a pleasant antidote to the general foppishness of wine events. Everybody seems to be wearing funny hats and buttons that say STAMP OUT WIMPY WINES. (Zins average almost 15 percent alcohol.) "Great juice, dude" is the highest compliment. The tasters often seem to forget to spit out the wine—as is customary with wine pros—so that after an hour or two, a certain hilarity prevails. A lot of the makers look suspiciously like surfers or computer geeks. At the booth for Schuetz Oles Zinfandel, unregenerate hippie winemaker Rick Schuetz identifies his main influences as Thelonious Monk, Jimi Hendrix, and Julia Child, while grape grower Russ Oles proclaims that his pals "all have names like Kippy, Cheech, and Shorty."

Francophiles and Anglo-style lovers of old-wine mellowness tend to be suspicious of the flamboyance of the typical high-alcohol, peppery, briery, jammy zinfandel. Silly hats aside, it's a big mistake to underestimate the seriousness of many of the new zins.

At least two producers—Turley Wine Cellars and Martinelli Vineyards—are currently crafting mind-boggling zinfandels that combine power and finesse and are among the best red wines I've tasted. Both operations have shared the consulting services of master winemaker Helen Turley (she left Turley after the '94 vintage to be replaced by her able and, incredibly, even taller assistant Ehren Jordan). Her brother, Turley Cellars proprietor Larry Turley, appears at first glance to be a typical zin dude, with his thick beard and laid-back, wide-grin demeanor, but he's also a practicing emergency room physician. He bottles several zinfandels, the most spectacular of which is the Hayne Vineyard. The first sip of the '94 is apt to shake and rattle you to your socks—like the first time you heard rock and roll *really* loud. "Jumpin' Jack Flash" comes to mind. Or maybe "Let's Spend the Night Together"—one of my notes from a tasting at the winery says: "Only sexual analogies can do justice." (For a good time call, or rather fax 707–963–8683.)

Martinelli's '94 Jackass Hill Vineyard zinfandel is, on the other hand, more "Layla" or "Free Bird" than "Jumpin' Jack." Same grape, similar-vintage old vines—and yet the style is *completely* different from Turley's. Jackass Hill has an incredibly velvety texture, in conjunction with a wild jungle of competing but somehow perfectly integrated dark-fruit flavors. One of my tasting notes says, "Free-range velvet." My comments after that are notable only by virtue of their numerous exclamation marks. "Blackberries! Smoke!" et cetera.

The Martinelli family (fax 707–525–WINE) has been growing grapes in Sonoma for more than a hundred years but only started bottling their own in 1993, guided by their winemaking genius Helen Turley. Good move. Great juice.

Both of these wines are limited in supply and hard to find, but there are dozens of good, small producers turning out delicious, inexpensive zinfandels, and the numbers are growing every year. Traditionally, longevity has been considered a prerequisite of a great wine: Good Bordeaux, for instance, acquires depth and character over the decades. Few of the zin producers I talked to pretended to be certain about how the wines will age, although decade-old examples of Ridge Vineyards are still going strong, and the Turleys and Martinellis from the '94 vintage are aging beautifully. The good news is that you can drink most zinfandels on release and leave the question of whether longevity equals greatness to the wine bores. They didn't think rock and roll would last either. And what could be more all-American than instant gratification?

GUERRILLAS IN THE HILLS
CULT CABERNETS

"There's gold in them there hills."
—Anon.
"There's hills in them there gold."
—Alfred Hitchcock, on seeing Grace Kelly in a gold lamé dress

Once upon a time, Napa cabs were to the wine world what IBM once was to the stock market—too obvious and ubiquitous to excite the interest of the maverick. (Like, big yawn, dude.) In just about the same span of time that Yahoo and Intel have become the new blue chips, the quality of Napa cabs has risen as fast as the Dow. A new generation has arrived to challenge the old guard: the Mondavi Reserves and the Heitz Martha's

Vineyards. And like the new post-Microsoft Internet stocks, boutique Cabernets (and cab blends) are springing up every year, creating a frenzy of interest at the auction houses and in the wine press. Unlike that fly-by-night.com you bought online yesterday, the quality of many of these wines is indisputable. It's undoubtedly premature to attempt a list of California first growths, as the Bordelaise did in 1855 when they created their controversial five-tier classification. But what the hell. *Impetuous* is my middle name.

The 1990s have witnessed a huge improvement in California winemaking, as well as an increased understanding of the importance of soil, microclimate, and viticulture. The multimillion-dollar phylloxera epidemic that swept Napa and Sonoma, thanks in part to rootstock advice from the boneheads—oops, sorry, make that eggheads—at U.C. Davis, has been a blessing in disguise, forcing older wineries to reevaluate where and how they plant. And newcomers have the benefit of past trials and errors. One common denominator of most of the great new Napa cult cabs is their location on hillsides, rather than on the valley floor.

"Even in ancient Rome," the *Oxford Companion to Wine* informs us, "it was said *Baccus amat colles,* or Bacchus loves the hills." Without going into a lot of boring stuff, let's just say that high-quality viticulture is counterintuitive: Whatever is good for corn is bad for wine. The supreme values of California culture—laid-back demeanor and constant sunshine—don't always make the best wine. Whatever doesn't kill your vines makes them stronger. You've got to stress the suckers. Hills are good for this. The soil is thin, the rocks are thick, the drainage is good and the temperatures, cool. And steep grades necessitate hand-picking, a boon for quality. Needless to say, these hillside wines are, almost by definition, limited in production.

Bill Harlan, a real estate investor with a serious wine jones, was one of those Californians who noticed that the great wines of Europe usually come from hillsides. Over the course of the 1980s he put together a precipitous hillside parcel on the west slope of the Napa Valley. Oblivious to the great views, his vines cling precariously to the slopes, thirsty and stressed to the max, like shantytown dwellers above Rio. With the help of Pomerol's flying wine wizard Michel Rolland, Harlan and winemaker Bob Levy have more than realized Harlan's goal of creating a great Bordeaux-like red, blending Cabernet with small amounts of Merlot, Cabernet Franc, and Petit Verdot. Anyone lucky enough to be on the mailing list, take note: I'll trade a '95 Château Mouton-Rothschild for a bottle of the '95 Harlan Estate. 'Nuff said.

Bryant Family Vineyard and Colgin Cellars are two other superstars of the past decade that come from Napa hillsides. Both were coaxed to fame by Helen Turley, who believes that serious slope and rocky soil are prerequisites for "Grand Cru" Napa sites. If we look at market price as an indicator of quality—as the Bordelaise did when they established their classification—these two wines, which can sell for upward of a thousand dollars a bottle at auction, are at the top of the Napa Valley hierarchy. And while both could be mistaken for monster hot-vintage first-growth Bordeaux, Turley's winemaking alchemy is such that they are far more delicious in their youth than their French counterparts. (On a personal note, the great '94 Colgin and '94 Bryant were on the table at the McInerney millennial dinner. If I were a better father, I would sell my modest holdings of both and secure my children's future.) The Turley-made Jayson Pahlmeyer Proprietary Red was also a serious contender for first-growth status, but Turley's recent departure as winemaker leaves the future in question.

Whether we measure by auction prices or Parker ratings, Dalla Valle is producing two of the greatest Napa reds. Their Cabernet Sauvignon and their Cabernet Franc blend named for their daughter, Maya, are spectacular wines from yet another great hillside location. Heidi Barrett, who consulted for Dalla Valle, is responsible for Screaming Eagle, one of the most recent of the hillside cult cabs, as well as Grace Family Vineyards, which was perhaps the first and remains the cultiest of them all. Add to this list the mighty Araujo Estate Wines Cabernet Sauvignon from the famous Eisele Vineyard, as well as Shafer Vineyards Hillside Select and Philip Togni Vineyard, and you've got the start of a Napa Valley first-growth classification. In addition to vineyard terrain that is inhospitable to corn and polo, these wines all have tiny production and huge prices in common.

NAPA'S OLD GUARD DIGS IN
CLASSIC CABS

Bacchus had come to town. And I was the last to hear. "Where's your glass?" asked Anne, the chestnut-tressed gamine standing in front of me in the line. She had shiny hazel eyes and the boneless demeanor of the righteously intoxicated. "You have to get a glass," her friend agreed. They promised to hold my place in the line while I trotted over to the other tent to secure, for five bucks, a special extra-large wineglass etched with the Silver Oak logo and filled with the latest ('95) vintage, officially being released that very day.

I had been on my way to visit another winery when I found my path through rural Oakville, in central Napa Valley, blocked by a Manhattan-style traffic jam. Hundreds of cars clogged the narrow lane between vineyards, and hundreds more were parked on either side. I saw a pack of vintage Harleys clustered behind a yellow Lamborghini, its sleek nose nuzzling the bumper of a Dodge minivan. From all directions streamed pilgrims with picnic baskets, boom boxes, and T-shirts that proclaimed LIFE IS A CABERNET. I had to check it out. I'm one-quarter Russian: If I see a line, I join it first and find out what's selling later.

I'd stumbled on the semiannual release of Silver Oak Cabernet Sauvignon, an event that's something like a cross between Woodstock and an Amway convention. When I returned to the queue, where the faithful were waiting to buy their allotment of Silver Oak, the girls were holding my place. Behind us, a retired couple from Minnesota said they had planned their trip to the Bay Area to coincide with this event, which they'd attended for the past four years. Over the course of the next hour I received invitations to visit people in many parts of the country. Phone numbers were exchanged. Glasses were refilled. "The great thing about this stuff," said Anne, swirling her glass and rotating her head to follow the movement of the ruby liquid, "is that it tastes so good, you can drink it all day and not get drunk." I'll only vouch for the first part of that statement.

Silver Oak is an anomaly, a large (fifty-thousand-case) producer with the status—and, many would say, the performance—of a cult winery. They now release two versions, the Napa Valley and the Alexander Valley. These are somewhat controversial in the wine community, not least, perhaps, because they taste so good upon release. There's still a perception that cabs are supposed to be mean and standoffish in their youth. As indeed many are. But I'm beginning to question this wisdom.

Almost without exception, the most famous Napa Valley Cabernet Sauvignon vineyards are on the benchland on the western side of the valley—in the regions of Oakville and Rutherford. The best are planted on alluvial gravel, which promotes drainage and somewhat discourages rampant growth. There's no question that great wines like Inglenook's '41, Heitz's Martha's Vineyard '74, and Mondavi's '87 Reserve have emerged from these vineyards. Still, one has to wonder whether early Napa Valley growers chose the flatland only out of convenience, and whether their successors can still compete at the highest level. In recent years smaller, low-production hillside vineyards like Bryant Family, Colgin Cellars, Dalla Valle, and Harlan Estate have stolen the thunder from the big boys on the flats. And what's more, these hillside mavericks are redefining the notion of what Napa Valley Cabernet is supposed to taste like. All of the above wines are superripe and super-concentrated; many are delicious at an early age.

The Quarterly Review of Wines, in a recent piece discussing Beaulieu Vineyard's famous Georges de Latour Private Reserve Cabernet Sauvignon, writes of "green olive and bell pepper" as the signature of Napa Valley Cabernet. Others have spoken of green bean and even broccoli scents and flavors. Personally, I think that vegetables have their place, but I don't want them throwing a party in my red-wine glass. I prefer the red and purple flavors, like currant and blackberry, and the secondary brown ones—coffee, chocolate, tobacco— that I find in a bottle of Bryant. (Mint and eucalyptus are also welcome.)

One reason most serious Cabernets need to be aged, aside from their tough tannins, is to give the salad bar elements time to be subsumed into the fruit. In the Cabernet-based wines of Bordeaux, the green flavors are often a function of underripeness. In warmer Napa Valley, with its longer growing season, I associate these green flavors with overproduction in valley floor vineyards. If the very first Napa cabs had been planted in the hills rather than in the valleys, I wonder if we wouldn't be unpleasantly surprised to find bell pepper in our glasses.

Driving around the valley floor, it's pretty easy to see who is likely to be making rich, concentrated, fruit-packed (that is, low-yield) wines. The best vineyards are severely pruned to prevent the greenery from stealing nutrients from the grapes, making them look rather like the yew hedges in old English gardens. Still, too many valley vineyards look like tree farms, riotous with greenery and loaded with grape bunches. No matter what happens in the cellar, great wines require low yields and fiercely disciplinary viticulture.

One of the old famous names I would still recommend is Mondavi; in fact, their '96 limited-release thirtieth-anniversary Napa Valley Cabernet is one of the greatest young reds I've ever tasted, as profound and subtle as a great young Pétrus. Its half sibling Opus One has become a consistent performer. In recent years Joseph Heitz seems to have lagged in quality, and I'm still waiting to be wowed by Sterling Vineyards. Georges de Latour Private Reserve, as I mentioned, is too salad-y for my taste, at least in its youth. Caymus Vineyard's famous Special Selection is usually good, although not always a great value at upward of $135 a bottle. Beringer's Cabernets are a good value at every price level. Dominus, owned by Christian Moueix of Pétrus fame, occupies part of the former Inglenook property and is superb. And Château Montelena remains one of the greatest Napa cabs after more than thirty years. All these wines are more widely available than their cultish cousins.

Right now I'd have to say that the guerrillas in the hills are winning the battle for first-growth status. But the counterattack has begun, and it looks fairly promising.

TOUGH LOVE
OREGON PINOT NOIR

Nobody ever said being in love with Pinot Noir is easy. At its silky, perfumy, French-speaking best, it is the most romantic grape of all. It's also thin skinned, temperamental, and provincial. One night it brings you close to heaven; the next you get slapped in the face. So maybe you blame it on the weather, which, in Burgundy, kind of sucks. "Maybe if we run away to a warmer place," you think . . . But take Pinot Noir to California and it often goes native in an alarming way, shedding its Gallic intellectual rigor and displaying a fruity, flirty, New World hedonism. Pinot Noir in a Hawaiian shirt and backward Phillies Blunt cap, quoting Marianne Williamson? "Honey, Jesus, no . . . this isn't what I meant at all . . ."

With some of these thoughts in mind, former dental school candidate David Lett drifted up to Oregon thirty-two years ago with a degree in viticulture and oenology from U.C. Davis and a seemingly quixotic belief that Oregon's Willamette Valley, with its long, cool growing season, was ideal for Pinot Noir. In 1980 his suspicions seemed to be verified by the results of a major tasting organized in the heart of Burgundy by Robert Drouhin. Lett's '75 Eyrie Vineyard Pinot Noir, South Block Reserve, came in second, by two-tenths of a point, to a '59 Chambolle-Musigny from the venerable Burgundian house of Drouhin. The Drouhins, no dummies, visited Oregon and eventually invested ten million dollars in a state-of-the-art winery up the hill from Eyrie. Drouhin is the exception: Most of Oregon's hundred-plus wineries are still undercapitalized, seat-of-the-pants operations. John Thomas, for instance, tends three and a half acres of Pinot Noir, does his own crushing and bottling, and delivers much of his production to Northwest buyers in his old Peugeot station wagon. Adelsheim Vineyard somehow manages to produce fine wine in an aboveground *chai* that is set into the side of a hill partially beneath the family dwelling; the day I visited the "cellar," the temperature was better suited to baking pizza than to making Pinot Noir.

Compared to imperial Napa, with its mansions and its multinational millions, Willamette is still a frontier. But with the excellent '93 and '94 vintages, Oregon Pinot Noir is coming into its own, and the town of McMinnville has become the Beaune of the New

World—site of the annual International Pinot Noir Celebration, where Pinot freaks from Australia to Auxey-Duresses gather every summer in August to celebrate their weird, difficult passion. Last summer David Lett presided over the tenth anniversary—a bearded, Papa Hemingway figure in a safari shirt. Such Burgundian giants as the Lacoste-shirted Comte Lafon and Domaine Dujac's elegant Jacques Seysses mingled democratically with their admirers. Californians who cruised north to catch the buzz included Jim Clenenden of Au Bon Climat, wearing—you guessed it—a Hawaiian shirt and backward cap, the David Lee Roth of the Pinot world. And yes, that *was* Beaux Frères winemaker Mike Etzel, with carrots in his ears— perhaps trying to entertain the French by imitating Jerry Lewis.

Festivalgoers discovered that Oregon Pinots are often better balanced and more Burgundian than their relatives from California. But they're usually more approachable and flirtatious than their French cousins, if not quite as perfumed. Still, there is a wide range of Willamette Valley styles, from the blockbuster "Is this a Châteauneuf-du-Pape?" kick of Beaux Frères to the daintier pleasures of the well-bred Domaine Drouhin. Lett, whose Eyries are lighter in color and body than most of the pack (and often awkward in their youth), fervently believes that the new kids are picking too late, achieving showy ripeness at the expense of true Pinot finesse and aging potential (basically, a tortoise-and-hare kind of argument). Tasting twenty of his older-vintage reserves dating back to 1970, I couldn't help admiring his achievement: The famed '75 was still brilliant, as were half a dozen of the older vintages. It's good to remember, as Lett insists, that Pinot Noir is traditionally valued for its delicacy and aromatic nuance. On the other hand, faced with, say, a lush, richly extracted bottle of '90 Domaine Serene Evenstad Reserve, it's tough to argue dogma. It's a little like complaining of a lover that he or she is too beautiful.

As in Burgundy, vintages are widely variable in Oregon. Some winemakers prefer the more delicate but balanced '93 vintage to the powerful super-ripe '94. The '95 and '96 vintages were less successful, and '97 was plagued by rains at harvesttime. Still, winemakers like Ken Wright managed to turn out some very good wines in these vintages. (In fact, I buy Ken Wright's wines in every vintage.) Fortunately, the gods smiled on the Willamette Valley in 1998. Conditions were perfect through most of the season as well as at harvest. Look for Adelsheim, Archery Summit, Broadleigh, Beaux Frères and its sibling Belles Soeurs, Brick House, Cristom, Ponzi, Thomas, Domaine Serene, and, of course, Ken Wright.

What you don't usually taste from Oregon is that hint of actual dirt that Burgundy freaks often believe to be the funky soul of their beloved—like sweat on a handkerchief—the deep, signature Côte d'Or grit, which can be as distinctive as the loamy growl of a real Delta bluesman. (Funny how French wines tend to possess the exact quality that their so-called popular music notoriously lacks.) Let's say that in recent years Oregon Pinot Noir has been a little like Clapton playing "Crossroads." It ain't exactly Robert Johnson. But it's more danceable. And the '98 vintage may well be Oregon's "Layla."

PINOT ENVY
SONOMA
PINOT NOIR

Like Thackeray's Becky Sharp or Marlene Dietrich in *The Blue Angel*, Pinot Noir has a way of making its admirers look foolish, and I have recently come to regret some generalizations I have made about California Pinot Noir. While most of Napa is too warm for Pinot, there are regions of California that seem to be proving themselves ideal: the foggy valleys of the central coast; Carneros; and western Sonoma. Although the notion of consistently excellent Pinot Noir has always seemed practically oxymoronic, like the concept of "safe sex," the Russian River Valley and the adjacent Sonoma coast region are turning out excellent Pinots with greater regularity than the climatically temperamental Willamette Valley or the Côte d'Or.

An epicurean English actor of my acquaintance was recently shocked to discover how much he preferred two Sonoma Pinots to a '94 Dominique Laurent Premier Cru from Nuits Saint-Georges. (Laurent is the hot, new big-oak kid on the Côte d'Or.) The Californians were '95 Marcassin and '95 Martinelli Reserve, both of which bear the stamp of alchemist Helen Turley. To be fair, I'd have to admit that the Nuits was too damn young, but given the continuing condescension of some of our friends across the Atlantic vis-à-vis American wines, I see no reason to be fair. With and without food, the Sonoma Pinots provided far more interest, fruit, and pleasure. And the Marcassin also showed more finesse. It has the knock-out power of ripe California fruit wrapped in a seamless velvet glove. Pinot Noir fanciers often feel they have to choose between the puppyishly friendly California style and the feline reserve of a Burgundy, but a wine like this makes you believe you can have it all.

Among the Pinot pioneers in western Sonoma is the Rochioli family, which has been growing grapes in the Russian River Valley since 1938; the fruit was sold off until 1982, when the family first began to produce an estate Pinot Noir. At about the same time, neighbors on Westside Road started the Williams & Selyem Winery, devoted almost entirely to the production of Pinot Noirs, including one made from Rochioli grapes that is one of the most sought-after bottles around. Both wineries have developed an almost fanatic following over the years, particularly for their small-production, single-vineyard Pinots, nearly all of which are sold through their mailing lists. Getting the top bottlings is a little like getting season tickets for the Knicks, but if you put yourself on the mailing list, both wineries can usually allocate a few bottles of their lesser offerings to you while you wait for the people higher on the list to die off. (Call Rochioli at 707–433–2305—March and October are its release dates; Williams & Selyem at 707–433–6425.) At the moment the best way to get some of these wines may be to find the select restaurants that carry them.

The world of California Pinot Noir lovers—a bigger fraternity than you'd think—was rocked by the announcement of the sale of Williams & Selyem in 1998. Many questioned the motives of new owner John Dyson, a former deputy mayor of New York City, who purchased little more than the name and a modest garage winery for some nine million dollars. (Williams & Selyem own no vineyards, relying on purchased grapes.) So loud was the keening and the gnashing of teeth that the *New York Times* jumped in to report on the sale at feature length. I haven't yet tasted the vintages made by new winemaker Bob Cabal. Fans of Burt Williams's handcrafted Pinots should look for the pre-'98 vintages, including the very successful '97. The new regime probably shouldn't be judged on the basis of the '98 vintage, which was a difficult one for Russian River Pinot. Perhaps the '99s will tell. In the meantime, seek out Rochioli. Their '97 Rochioli Vineyard is voluptuous and complex, like a Clos Saint-Denis from a super-ripe year.

The Martinelli family has been growing grapes in the Russian River Valley since the turn of the century. They didn't start bottling Pinot until 1993, when winemakers Steve Ryan and Helen Turley came aboard (fax 707–525–WINE). Kistler (707–823–5603), Dehlinger (707–823–2378), and Rabbit Ridge (707–431–7128) also bottle fine Russian River Pinots. A little to the north, Joan and William Smith, of W. H. Smith, have been producing superb Sonoma Pinot Noir since 1992 (fax 707–965–0324).

In 1985 Helen Turley and her husband, John Wetlaufer, bought what they believed to be the perfect vineyard site on a remote Sonoma coast ridge, some eleven hundred feet above sea level. After producing some of the most renowned Chardonnays and Cabernets in California (Colgin, Bryant Family, Pahlmeyer), Turley and Wetlaufer could have found any number of outside investors for their Pinot project. However, not wanting to cede control to anyone less maniacally devoted to quality, they lived like grad students for years while saving their earnings to develop the site. Birds ate most of the grapes before the first harvest, in 1995, which in the end yielded just a single barrel of Pinot Noir. But the few who have tasted it are rapturous. For the '96 vintage, Turley and Wetlaufer purchased expensive nets to fend off the birds. Remarkably, the wine is even more spectacular. The '99, which I recently tasted in barrel, may turn out to be the greatest vintage to date. (Drinking it is like performing a sexual act that involves silk sheets,

melted dark chocolate, and black cherries, while the
mingled scent of cinnamon, coffee, and cola wafts
though the air.) As good as the Pinots from this region
have been in the past, their Marcassin may raise the bar.

A large number of these Sonoma Pinots are released in the spring. Perhaps this is the place to
mention that many of the best wines in America today—cabs, zins, and chards as well as Pinots—are
available only via mailing lists and that it is illegal for
private individuals to receive wine shipments in most
states of the union. Grape nuts outside the states of
California and Oregon sooner or later have to choose
between their respect for the laws of their state and
their desire to imbibe the best. Fire up a Cohiba and
read Thoreau's "Civil Disobedience" while you mull it
over. Here's a tip, though: I don't know any producers
who ship in boxes that feature the *W* word.

WHO YOU CALLING PETITE?
PETITE SIRAH

I recently leased a Chevy Suburban for the summer. Navigating a parking lot in Nashville, Tennessee, while talking on the mobile phone, I failed to notice a curb, which had been inconveniently constructed between two adjacent lots, until I was crossing it. Fortunately the Suburban, which stands about twenty feet tall, treated the inconvenient obstruction as if it were a twig, and if not for the startled reactions of some passersby, I might not have noticed my mistake. A few days later I was consuming a steak au poivre at Balthazar in downtown Manhattan with '96 Granite Springs Petite Sirah, which a friend had brought along, when it occurred to me that Petite Sirah is the four-wheel-drive, off-road vehicle of the wine world. Steak au poivre has always been a problem for wine lovers, overwhelming your mature Bordeaux, let alone your young Pinot Noir. A tough young Syrah or Cabernet can sometimes maintain its identity in the face of fatty, spicy meat. But Petite Sirah, with its fierce tannins and its peppery highlights, rolls right over those peppercorns, taming and even complementing a pepper steak or a blackened fish.

To clear up some confusion at the start—Petite Sirah is not Syrah, and it's definitely not petite, although some winemakers add to the confusion by spelling it *Petite Syrah*. No one really knows where the name came from, or for that matter the grape itself. In fact, there's some dispute about whether it exists. Something called Petite Sirah has been growing in California for more than a century. The vines were often interspersed with zinfandel in older vineyards. Until recently it was considered a rough and unglamorous grape, used primarily to beef up blended reds and lighter varietals like zinfandel and even Cabernet Sauvignon. But the firms of Louis M. Martini and Ridge experimented with Petite Sirah in the 1970s and were soon followed by mavericks like Sean Thackrey and David Bruce. The grape gained some respectability when Thackrey's '92 Sirius was named best red wine of 1996 by *The Wine Enthusiast*. Unfortunately, Thackrey lost his lease on the Petite Sirah vineyard from which he made the wine.

The tiny Granite Springs Winery was founded in 1980 in El Dorado County; its Petite Sirah has become

one of the benchmarks for the varietal. Winemaker
Craig Boyd seems to have a natural affinity for Petite
Sirah, although a decade ago he could barely tell the
difference between Cabernet and Chardonnay. As an
engineer for Westinghouse, he was frequently called
upon to entertain clients. Early in his career the arrival
of the wine list was a scary moment—"At that point
my experience had been Riunite and Almaden"—but
gradually it became for him the main event. Fed up
with the nuclear-power industry, he was accepted to
the winemaking school at U.C. Davis in 1989 and
started working as an assistant at Granite Springs in
1991. By that time the winery's Petite Sirah had developed a cult following. Rather like the Côte-Rôtie producers who add small amounts of delicate Viognier (a
white grape) to their Syrah, Boyd, who likes big wine,
adds up to 10 percent Syrah. It tells you something
about the power of Petite Sirah that Syrah, a powerful
grape itself, might be considered a mellowing agent.
"It's always a big, bold, tannic wine," Boyd says of PS.
"I love the black pepper and spice character." Boyd
likes to drink it with anything involving pepper. And he
claims it's the ultimate Thanksgiving wine, by virtue of
having the power to stand up to any of the side dishes.

The most profound Petite Sirahs I've tasted come
from Turley Wine Cellars (they spell it *Syrah*),
renowned for its zinfandels. Until 1994 the wine was
made by the legendary Helen Turley, who happens to
be the sister of proprietor Larry Turley. When I blind-
tasted the '94 Hayne Vineyard PS in 1996, I couldn't

imagine what it was. It looked pretty much like india ink, with a slightly purple hue. In the mouth it was massive, searingly tannic (tannins are the astringent preservative agents found in grape skins, seeds, and stalks), and somewhat reminiscent of black licorice. Tasted later with a richly marbled steak, it began to show its genius. I can't explain the chemistry, but tannin and animal fat—unlike media properties—have an essentially synergistic reaction. I bought a case of this wine, and I'm happy to report that it's developing beautifully. Since 1995 the wine has been made by Turley's former protégé Ehren Jordan, who reports that the Petite Sirahs from the Hayne and Aida Vineyards, planted in 1946 and 1917 respectively, sell out even faster than the famous Turley zinfandels. (Both varietals are severely rationed by mailing list.) Turley Wine Cellars purchase just one-fifth of the Petite Sirah grapes in the Hayne Vineyard; the rest is used to beef up some of Napa's top Cabernets. Jordan recommends PS with wild boar, which sounds about right. (He and owner Larry Turley, the tallest team in the wine business, hunt them together.) Definitely an off-road wine.

Among the other benchmarks for this varietal are La Jota Vineyard, David Bruce, De Loach, and Ridge Vineyards York Creek bottling. Jordan recommends the PS made by Richard Aubert under the Rockland label. None of these wines is made in vast quantities. Currently there are about twenty-seven hundred acres of Petite Sirah vineyards in California, and much of the production disappears into blends. In the meantime, oenologists are trying to figure out what it is. In a recent study of so-called Petite Sirah vineyards by Carole Meredith at U.C. Davis, most contained vines that were genetically identical to Durif, a nearly extinct French varietal; others tested out as another obscure French grape called Peloursin. Like Bigfoot, another burly West Coast native, there seems to be some doubt about its very existence. But I've tasted it, and I'm a believer.

MERLOT: LUXURIOUS? OR LAME?

Merlot is the secret weapon of Bordeaux's Pomerol region, the grape that makes Château Pétrus among the most powerful, expensive, and sought-after red wines in the world. It's also the grape responsible for the most insipid red wines of the New World—the white zinfandel of the 1990s, Muzak for your palate. The average Merlot is so wimpy it's hard to believe it even contains alcohol.

Tasters inevitably use the words *fleshy, silky,* and *opulent* to describe the flavor and texture of Pétrus and the Merlot-based wines of Pomerol, as if they were describing the later paintings by Rubens. Velvet is frequently invoked. (I sometimes suspect that the power of suggestion may be at work in this case, since most of us read about Pétrus long before we taste it, and read about it *more* than we taste it.) The great Robert Parker detects "a lush, voluptuous, almost unctuous texture" and adds, "All are a result of the Merlot grape." Well, okay. I've been lucky enough to taste six vintages of the big *P*, and I was never less than impressed. The '61 is one of the best wines ever to touch my lips. But those of us whose net worth is unknown to *Forbes* magazine may wonder if it is possible to experience this alleged opulence for less than a thousand dollars a bottle—which is about what the '95 or the '98 Pétrus will set you back, if you can find either. Its tiny neighbor Le Pin is difficult to find at any price. Is it only in the clay of Pomerol (and, to a lesser extent, Saint-Émilion) that Merlot becomes synonymous with luxury?

In the traditional blend of grapes used in the Médoc region of Bordeaux, Cabernet Sauvignon was Lennon to Merlot's McCartney; cab provided the guts, Merlot brought a bit of lyrical finesse. Merlot ripened earlier and had fewer of the bitter tannins, which provide age-worthiness and structure but can be forbidding in a young wine. The ideal in Bordeaux is more or less to mix "Yer Blues" and "Lovely Rita" so that you come up with something like "A Day in the Life." Following the French lead, some California producers planted small plots of Merlot to help mellow their cabs.

Back in the early 1970s, when California Cabernets were often tough and tannic to a fault, the people at Louis M. Martini and Sterling Vineyards experimented with separately vinifying some Merlot plantings. (*Mellow* coincidentally, being the buzzword of that period.) The results inspired others—Duckhorn being among the most notable early producers (though I'm not impressed with recent vintages). Consumers responded to the kinder, gentler new varietal on the block, and growers started planting it wherever they could.

"If the bottle says 'Merlot,' it's easy to sell," says Susie Selby, whose burly Selby Merlot would probably surprise the average Merlot drinker. "Soft" is the virtue ascribed to the grape by its fans. But as anyone who has slept on a bad mattress can tell you, soft is not necessarily good. America's favorite new red wine reminds me of the lesser songs of Wings. If you liked "Let 'Em In" and "Silly Love Songs," you'll probably love Forest Glen Merlot.

Actually, in the wrong soil and the wrong hands, Merlot is worse than soft; it's thin and vegetal. In Bordeaux winemakers have had hundreds of years to match grapes to soil and microclimate, and it will be many years before the map of northern California is similarly parsed. Meantime, we know that cool sites are preferred. The most luxurious American Merlot comes from Washington's cool Columbia Valley: Leonetti Cellars' Merlot possesses that elusive, fleshy, silky texture so often ascribed to the great Pomerols, though its tiny production makes it rarer than Le Pin.

A recent trip to Napa and Sonoma as well as a blind tasting of fifteen premium Merlots have convinced me of two things: 1. There *is* such a thing as luxurious

California Merlot; 2. there is *no* such thing as a good, cheap California Merlot; most have a big, gaping hole in the middle where the fruit should be. If you want a round, fruity red for ten dollars, buy a '98 Côtes du Rhône. Serious California Merlot, like the Neyers Vineyards Merlot Napa Valley, starts at about twenty-five dollars a bottle.

My candidate for the Pétrus of Napa would be the Pahlmeyer Merlot, crafted by consulting winemaker Helen Turley. Her powerful '94, '95, and '97 belie the image of Merlot as easy-listening music for the palate. Pahlmeyer is among the very few wines made by Turley that is actually available at retail around the country.* Turley is such a perfectionist that I imagine her vines standing nervously at attention when she visits the vineyards. Fortunately, a few others are whipping this flabby grape into shape, like Selene's Mia Klein, an intense Hermosa Beach native (is that an oxymoron?) who also makes a brilliant Sauvignon Blanc.

Very few California Merlots will bear comparison with the '98 Pomerols, let alone Pétrus and Le Pin. And it's worth noting that Pétrus's Christian Moueix produces a Cabernet-based wine at Dominus Estate, his California winery. A handful of the new Californians represent an affordable luxury: the vinous equivalent of sevruga. If you are looking for beluga, whip out your Gold Card and call for Bordeaux.

---

*Helen Turley parted company with Pahlmeyer in the fall of 1999.

BIG RED MONSTER FROM DOWN UNDER
SHIRAZ

What will you have to drink?" the steward asked shortly after I had boarded a Quantas jet in Los Angeles, bound for Sydney. It being 11:00 A.M., I requested a Perrier. He raised his eyebrows and frowned at me: "Oh, dear," he said. "You're not going to be much fun." I was reminded of the old Monty Python sketch about the Australian philosophy department, where Rule Number One was "No not drinking." (This was also Rule Number Three.) A couple of hours later, when I requested a glass of Aussie Riesling with my lunch, the same steward shook his head. "Not the Riesling," he said. "No?" I asked. "Go with the Sémillon," he insisted. And by God, he was right. At suppertime, just past Hawaii, when I asked for the

Cabernet, the fastidious steward-sommelier directed me to the Shiraz. If only I had not been so diligent about observing Rule Number One, I might still remember the name of it. Anyway, take my word, it was great.

After a week in Australia—during which I never laid eyes on a vineyard—I concluded that Shiraz is the great Australian grape. And I decided that—besides the cheap wines with which I'd been familiar in the States—the Australians are turning out some spectacular premium wines.

Shiraz (known as Syrah elsewhere) is a warm-weather grape well suited to the temperate zones of southern Australia. Though it may seem absurd to generalize, the typical Australian Shiraz bounds up and introduces itself with a slap on your back, sticks a pot of jam in your nose, then offers to put you up for the night and lend you money. As opposed to the standoffish Rhône Valley Syrah, which usually takes years to open up and address you by your given name.

Until the introduction of cuttings from the Cape of Good Hope in 1791, there had been no vines in Australia. A century later vineyards in South Australia, Victoria, and New South Wales were slaking the heroic thirsts of an ever-expanding population of ex-convicts and their descendants while providing thousands of barrels of rustic fortified wines for export to the righteous souls in England. This high-octane plonk, I like to imagine, wreaked a measure of headachy revenge on the exiles' former prosecutors in the motherland. In recent years the evolution of the Australian wine industry has somewhat resembled that of the Californian. An increasing demand for dry table wines, as well as indigenous technological innovations—not to mention a subsequent antitechnology backlash—have resulted in a quantum leap in quality since the 1950s. And while several large Gallo-like operations control a huge part of the market, there has been, as in Napa and Sonoma, an explosion of boutique wineries and an increasing emphasis on premium wines.

Wine buffs in Europe and the States have long been familiar with Grange Hermitage, first introduced in the 1950s and now known simply as Penfold's Grange. Modeled on the Syrah-based Hermitage of France's northern Rhône, this now famous wine raised the standard for a grape that had previously been regarded Down Under as a lowly workhorse, and introduced the radical notion of world-class Australian wine. In good years it is as rich and complex as almost any red wine on the planet and can taste as much like a Château Latour as a great Chave Hermitage. It's now released at about $120 a bottle in the States, and it doesn't linger on the shelves. (Fortunately, Penfold's makes excellent, less expensive Shirazes.) Almost as highly regarded by the locals is Henschke's Hill of Grace, another highly concentrated and age-worthy Shiraz. A third contender for Big Monster from Down Under has recently emerged: Astralis, which, with the possible exception of Turley Hayne Vineyard Petite Syrah, is the most extracted, inky, macho red wine I have ever encountered. If you've got plenty of cash, durable enamel on your teeth, and the patience to wait ten years, I highly recommend it. Eat it with smoked kangaroo or perhaps grilled *Tyrannosaurus rex* steaks rubbed with chili.

Unlike Grange, a product of the massive Penfold's conglomerate, Astralis is made at the tiny Clarendon Hills Winery, located twenty-five miles southeast of Adelaide. Clarendon also makes slightly larger quantities of a refined and inexpensive Clarendon Hills Shiraz (as well as an old-vine Grenache for which I would gladly trade some of the off-vintage Château Rayas in my cellar). Fortunately for American consumers, Clarendon's wines are now available in the States, along with those of a number of other small-production, artisanal estates, through the Australian Premium Wine Collection, brainchild of Dublin-born businessman–bon viveur John Larchet, who visited Australia on a *Wanderjahr* in 1981 and, partly out of enthusiasm for the wines he discovered there, was unable to pry himself away. When planning his Chicago wedding, Larchet discovered that it was almost impossible to find small-production premium wines from Australia, so he decided to start his own import company.

Although the Australian Premium Wine Collection includes most of the grape varietals grown in regions of his adopted land, Larchet believes that Shiraz, in its any variations, is the most expressive Australian red. There are now dozens of well-made, powerful, spicy, complex, meat-friendly Aussie Shirazes in the twenty-five-dollar range (the Barossa Valley is an especially good source), which provide far more value and drinking satisfaction than some of the lesser Rhônes or the midrange California Syrahs. Not necessarily for the Chambolle-Musigny and chamber-music fans among us, Australian Shiraz very often tastes like it comes from the same country that brought us the music of AC/DC, a band that emphatically subscribed to Rule Number One.

SUMMER REDS

All wine would be red," said the late Leon Adams, "if it could." While I'm not convinced that the Domaine de la Romanée-Conti's '95 Montrachet feels socially inferior when it bumps into a bottle of Beaujolais Nouveau on the streets of Beaune, I can sympathize with Adams's sentiment. Many drinkers think of white wine as foreplay and feel somehow unsatisfied with a meal that doesn't lead eventually to red. Which is why, though summer undoubtedly has many features to recommend it—hot weather, tiny bathing suits, long days—some of us can't help dreading it as the doldrums of the red-wine drinker's year. It's hard to think about opening that big old bottle of Beaucastel or Beychevelle when you're sweating like a . . . I was about to say *pig,* but in fact, as my animal-mad wife has reminded me, pigs don't sweat. Sweating like a horse, maybe. Whatever. Anyway, I'm happy to report that some red wines go well with suntan lotion.

The key to summertime reds is temperature control. Most start to lose focus above sixty-five degrees, and sixty-two degrees is probably closer to ideal. Sommelier Daniel Johnnes at New York's Montrachet recommends that lighter reds—that is, summer reds—be served at between fifty-six and fifty-eight degrees. This suggests that, when the temperature is in the eighties, wines like Beaujolais and Sancerre *rouge* should spend ten minutes in the ice bucket before being served. But don't overdo it; below fifty-five degrees you won't taste much of anything.

I don't drink much Beaujolais in the colder months, but it fills a niche at the beach. Made from the prolific and exuberant Gamay grape and grown on the granite hills of lower Burgundy, it's fruity, friendly, and cheap— a Hawaiian shirt of a wine. Generic Beaujolais may be too simple—it's worth the extra buck or so to step up to Beaujolais-Villages. Richer still are the Beaujolais crus, which bear the names of their villages—Brouilly, Côte de Brouilly, Fleurie, Chénas, Morgon, Juliénas, Régnié, Chiroubles, Saint-Amour, and Moulin-à-Vent. I'm partial to Brouilly, which seems to be all anyone drinks in the bistros of Paris. Ready for swilling, the '99 vintage is good if overabundant. But, hey, we're just trying to have some fun here.

Georges Duboeuf and Louis Jadot are the top *né-gotiants,* but it's worth seeking out some of the smaller growers whose wines are more subtle—makers like Domaine de Vissoux (Beaujolais), Alain Michaud (Brouilly), Château Thivin (Côte de Brouilly), Michel Tete (Juliénas), and Jacky Janodet (Moulin-à-Vent). The big news out of Beaujolais is coming from growers in Morgon and Fleurie, the so-called Gang of Five— Jean Foillard, Marcel Lapierre, Guy Breton, Yvon Mètras, and Jean-Paul Thèvenet. What makes these guys renegades in the eyes of their neighbors is their dedication to low yields, natural yeasts, minimal fining—that is, clarification—and filtration. In short, they are making Beaujolais as if it were real wine. What a concept. For that very reason, you may want to save these wines for the cooler weather in early fall.

Much of my summer drinking budget goes to growers of Burgundy's famed Côte d'Or, to the north of Beaujolais, where Pinot Noir rules. The lesser Burgundies of '97—a good vintage in Burgundy, as in most of the world—are perfect for drinking with grilled chicken and fish. Or by themselves. Look for Côte-de-Nuits-Villages from the top makers—like the impeccable Domaine de l'Arlot—as well as the village wines of Givry, Maranges, Marsannay, Santenay, and Mercurey. Closer to home, the lighter-styled Pinots from the Russian River Valley and the central coast of California also make good summer drinking. I particularly like Calera's central-coast Pinot Noir.

Barolo and Barbaresco are out of the question in hot weather; the Piedmontese equivalent of Beaujolais is Dolcetto (named, unlike the big *B*s, for its grape rather than its turf). My current favorite is Marcello and Bruno Ceretto's gorgeous '98 Dolcetto D'Alba Rossana. A dry but fruity, early-maturing wine, it seems, like all Italian wine, to be very good with food, as does Barbera—one of the very few red wines that stand up to the acidity of tomato sauce. The best Barolo and Barbaresco makers are usually the best sources for both of these wines; in addition to Ceretto, I like Pio Cesare, Aldo Conterno, and the great Angelo Gaja. Harder to find in this country is Grignolino, a fragrant, pale red varietal that is the summer quaff of many Piedmontese winemakers.

The Loire Valley is best known for its crisp, dry white wines, but it also produces red wines, many of which scream to be drunk in the summer. Chinon, in the central Loire Valley, produces sprightly Cabernet Franc–based reds. Beloved of native son Rabelais, Chinon is an exuberant wine that often seems sharpest after a dip in the ice bucket. Look for Joguet, Baudry, and Raffault.

When dining out, you may get a disapproving look from your waiter as you order an ice bucket for your Dolcetto or your Beaujolais. Just to compound his confusion, order the fish. What the hell, summer's the time for cheap thrills.

A RIVALRY MADE IN HEAVEN
LAFITE AND MOUTON

When he bought Château Lafite in 1868, Baron James Rothschild may have been trying to trump his English cousin Nathaniel de Rothschild, who'd bought the adjacent estate of Mouton fifteen years earlier, but I suspect his real intent was to make life easier for future wine critics. Like Tolstoy and Dostoevsky, like Borg and McEnroe, Lafite-Rothschild and Mouton-Rothschild, the two most famous red wines in the world, are a dichotomy made in heaven.

In terms of sheer brand-name recognition, Lafite is first among equals, although fame doesn't necessarily equate with popularity in this elitist realm. If there were the equivalent of a Pepsi challenge, Mouton would probably win the popular vote. Lafite is exactly the kind

of wine that can make the amateur enthusiast feel defi-
cient in judgment—that makes him wonder if he just
doesn't "get it." I definitely didn't get it the first four
or five times I tried Lafite. It was like listening to Haydn
with my parents. Whereas my first sip of Mouton was a
little like hearing Nirvana on *Saturday Night Live*.

Lafite and Mouton are among five officially classified Bordeaux "first growths" (although Mouton was
not elevated to that status until 1973, the only significant alteration of the 1855 classification). Both wines
are from the commune of Pauillac—also home of
Château Latour—and both share certain secondary
characteristics, including, usually, a whiff of cedar and,
sometimes, strange as it may seem, the smell of freshly
sharpened lead pencils. (I've never noticed this in any
other wine.) Both become more complex over the years
and can, in great vintages, last almost forever. And both
have had disappointing stretches. Lafite turned out
weak wines during the 1960s and early 1970s, while
Mouton had a slump in the late 1980s and early 1990s.

You probably know, even if you have never tasted
them, that Lafite is synonymous with elegance,
Mouton with power. Lafite is fragrant and ethereal,
Mouton loud and fleshy. Lafite is Leonardo to
Mouton's Michelangelo. If they made clothes, Lafite
would be Armani and Mouton, Versace. "If Lafite was
an artist, it would be Chagall," Eric Rothschild once
told me. "If a musician—Mozart." And as if these
stereotypes weren't stark enough, a visit to the two
wineries will absolutely confirm them.

Mouton is the major tourist destination in the Médoc, one of the slickest winery tours in the world. All in all it reminds me of Robert Mondavi's Napa Valley winery—not so surprising when you consider that Baron Philippe de Rothschild and the great Napa Valley booster joined forces years ago to create the Franco-American Opus One. The slide show that initiates a tour of Mouton is both arty *and* techy—simultaneous images of grapes, vines, and oak barrels projected on two screens and one revolving disco ball. Lighting in the cellars is theatrical, clearly designed for the visitor's pleasure as much as for the worker's convenience. The museum, devoted to art with vinous themes, sounds kitschy, but turns out to be an impressive monument to the taste of the late Baron Philippe, the flamboyant aristocrat who inherited Mouton in the 1920s and devoted much of his considerable energy to improving and promoting it. His legacy is carried on by his daughter Philippine, who also seems to be an extrovert and an enthusiast, judging from my brief encounters.

Lafite is a very different experience for the visitor. In fact, visitors are not encouraged—I had to beg an appointment through my friend Bruno Borie, whose family owns Ducru Beaucaillou. Eric Rothschild, the debonair proprietor, was in Paris when I was shown around by the manager of the estate. The only dramatic aspect of Lafite is the Ricardo Bofill–designed circular cellar—a half-submerged Pantheon that's apparently very functional. But the explanation of the vinification sounded almost exactly like that at

Mouton. No expense is spared. In the past Lafite spent far more time in barrel than Mouton, which partly accounted for its more repressed style, but now the differences in barrel time are minimal.

So if they are so different, why are they different—the wines of these two neighboring estates? There's the tempting personality fallacy: Baron Philippe was flamboyant, ditto his wines. There's the grape theory, that Mouton has a higher proportion of Cabernet Sauvignon—the John Lennon of the grape world—while Lafite uses slightly more of the McCartney-like Merlot. (Although in recent vintages the final blend of Lafite has had a very high proportion of Cabernet.) The third theory, the *terroir* theory, goes to the heart of the French classification system. It's all in the dirt, or, as is more the point here, in the rocks—in a thousand minute variables of geology and topography and meteorology. While both have the heavy riverine gravels that make for good drainage, Mouton has more iron and sandstone just underneath; Lafite has more limestone.

In recent years some observers have remarked that the differences between various Bordeaux properties, including Lafite and Mouton, have become more muted, blaming 1. technological advances, 2. later picking, and 3. the influence of a certain American wine critic who likes big, powerful wines. And it does seem true that Lafite, especially in a vintage like '96, has become a bolder and more buxom wine. Not necessarily a bad thing given how positively shy and dainty some of the old ones were. On the other hand, I recently tasted both '99s at the châteaux and they seemed completely in character—that is, very different. I'm betting that *terroir*, like breeding, will reveal itself in the long run. What these great stubborn wines have always had in common is the ability to last and to improve for decades, developing a staggering range of nuances. If you've got the cash, the patience, and the life expectancy, track down the excellent '95 or '96 vintages of these wines. And then forget about them for ten or fifteen years.

SAINT-ESTEPHE
STEPS OUT

The proprietor of a venerable Bordeaux château doesn't entirely approve of my plan to visit Haut-Marbuzet. "He's a socialist," the man says of Henri Duboscq, the co-owner and winemaker of the Cru Bourgeois Saint-Estèphe estate. Other Bordelais disapprove not so much of Duboscq's politics as of his winemaking, which they judge to be too flamboyant. *Sexy* and *exotic* are among the words used to describe the wines of Haut-Marbuzet, and one gets the feeling that this is not quite *comme il faut* for Bordeaux; it's as if a bikini-clad Juliette Binoche crashed a meeting of the French Academy. Duboscq's style is particularly anomalous in Saint-Estèphe, the northernmost commune of the Médoc, which has long been the least sexy of them all.

When, after a drive through the gently rolling hills of Saint-Estèphe, I arrive at Haut-Marbuzet, I'm greeted by Bruno Duboscq, Henri's young, Michael J. Fox–like son, who seems positively wholesome, preppy, and eager to please. He explains that the HM style is in part a result of late picking, as he shows me the old concrete fermentation vats—"just like Pétrus"—and the rows of new-oak barrels. My eyes always glaze over when the talk turns to specs of vinification. But tasting is another matter. After the tour, the glasses come out. The '90 is positively Baudelairean in its decadent pleasures, and more-recent vintages are nearly as good. Whatever they're doing, it works.

Haut-Marbuzet often resembles a rich Châteauneuf-du-Pape like Beaucastel or even a Grand Cru Burgundy from a very ripe year. "We try to minimize the traditional hardness of the Saint-Estèphe *terroir*," Bruno says, "so that the wines drink well when they're young." I'm so taken that I buy a case of the '95 directly from the on-site office to lug back on the plane. A dislocated shoulder seems like a small price to pay for the pleasure of being the first on my block to own this precocious and opulent beverage. More than half of Haut-Marbuzet's populist wines are sold directly to the public, who drive in from all over Europe to load up their trunks with the latest vintage.

Once viewed as the dowdy sibling of communes like Pomerol and Pauillac, Saint-Estèphe has been coming into its own of late. (It's also the prettiest part of the Médoc, reminding me of Vermont.) In his classic *Bordeaux,* Robert M. Parker Jr. says that the wines of Saint-Estèphe "have the reputation of being the slowest to mature, and the toughest, most tannic wines." This is in part a result of the heavy soil, with its high clay content. Dark plum and tea are among the characteristic flavors. Only five Saint-Estèphe properties were included in the 1855 classification, and until recently, several of those were underperforming. But the '96 vintage serves as confirmation of the progress made in this commune in recent years, in part because Saint-Estèphe received less rainfall that year than did the more venerable communes to the south.

No property has been more influential in the awakening of sleepy Saint-Estèphe than Cos (pronounced to rhyme with *boss*) d'Estournel (rhymes with Lester Bell) the super second growth, which was nurtured to greatness by Bruno Prats. The bizarre Chinese/Indian–style folly of a château, built in the nineteenth century by eccentric Asia-phile Louis Gaspard d'Estournel, is the first notable feature of the Saint-Estèphe landscape as one crosses the border from Pauillac on the D2. For the past twenty years Cos has been the undisputed star of the region, producing one of the best wines of Bordeaux. The signature toughness of Saint-Estèphe is tempered here by a high proportion of Merlot grapes, which soften and round out the wine—a strategy that is lately being used elsewhere in the commune.

For many years Château Montrose was considered the greatest of Saint-Estèphes. The wines of the 1950s and 1960s were made in a massive, long-lived style that reminded many of Latour. In the 1970s and early 1980s an attempt was made to lighten up the wine, with results that suggested Aleksandr Solzhenitsyn in a tutu or maybe Bob Dole flacking for Viagra. But Robert Parker's hundred-point rating for the '90 vintage signaled a recent return to classic form. Montrose is not a wine for early drinking, but it's usually worth the wait. The same is true of third-growth Calon-Ségur, a classic late-blooming Saint-Estèphe that has the virtue of wearing a heart on its label.

From the consumer's point of view, the best news from Saint-Estèphe is the large number of unclassified Cru Bourgeois properties turning out excellent and affordable wine. My favorite of these for many years has been Château Meyney, consistently one of the best values in Bordeaux for those who have the patience to cellar it—always a big meaty mouthful, with a black licorice signature. Also look for Lafon-Rochet, Lilian Ladouys, de Pez, Les Ormes de Pez, Cos Labory, Lavillotte, Phélan Ségur, and the aforementioned Haut-Marbuzet. Most of these wines are available in the twenty- to thirty-dollar range, and given the nasty price increases for this very good but not outstanding vintage, they're among the few '96 Bordeaux that will land in my cellar.

BORDEAUX ON
A BUDGET

Just when you thought Bordeaux prices couldn't get any more ridiculous—just when you thought the crash of the Asian economies was going to put an end to the days when Château Pétrus was being served with Coke in Hong Kong—down comes word that the dubious '97s are being released at prices that are about 20 percent higher than the far more promising '96s. I was in Bordeaux for the '97 harvest, and I'm certainly not amused. The legendary spinmeisters who own the châteaux and sell the wines—whose notorious enthusiasm for their current vintage can make James Carville appear, by comparison, to be nonpartisan—even they had a hard time hiding their skepticism and confusion about the vintage, which was characterized by uneven flowering and uneven ripening of the grapes. (The harvest stretched out over a month at some châteaux; grapes that looked like peas were hanging next to grapes that looked like raisins.) I wish I could say my first visit to Bordeaux coincided with the vintage of the century, but I don't think so. Meantime, the excellent '95 vintage has risen sharply in price since its release.

In 1855 the wine brokers of Bordeaux created the famous classification, which ranked sixty-one wines from first to fifth growth, and the prices for these wines have been rising ever since. I can already hear myself someday trying to explain to my daughter as we sit in the twilight sharing a bottle of Romanian Cabernet Franc how classed Bordeaux—the stuff ranked first through fifth growth—was a beverage that was once bought and consumed by ordinary mortals. I was engaged in this gloomy speculation when I recalled a dinner at Sparks Steak House in Manhattan some years ago with Frank Prial, the *New York Times* wine columnist, at which, if I recall correctly, he had been speaking favorably about the second labels of the first-growth châteaux. Or maybe he was just commending Les Forts de Latour in particular, the second wine of famed Château Latour, which we had quite a bit of that night, hence the imprecision of my memory.

Like other second labels, it's made from the produce of younger vines and vats that are judged not quite powerful enough for the *grand vin*. Aside from its lower price, it has the virtue of making accessible the famously backward and masculine Latour style years before the *grand vin* will be drinkable. In the best years—like '82, '89, '90, and '95—it's a very good bet. Château Margaux, another first growth, has been bottling its second label, Le Pavillon Rouge du Château Margaux, since 1908. These two wines have long been a secret of budget-minded connoisseurs.

In the past decade or so second-label wines—not to be confused with second *growths*—have proliferated; there are now dozens to choose from, not only from the first-growth producers but also from properties that were ranked second, third, and even fifth growth in the somewhat outdated 1855 classification. Theoretically, this is a happy development, at least for purchasers of the primary label or *grands vins,* the idea being that the first wine of any given maker is improved by virtue of strict barrel selection; wine that is not quite up to snuff is siphoned off to the second label. The question is, how good is the remaining juice—technically, let's face it, the dregs—which is bottled under the second label? And the answer is—good question. In weaker years, '91 through '94 for instance, the second-label wines, if they were made, were apt to contain underripe or dilute grapes. (The more scrupulous makers declassify and sell this wine off in bulk.) In a year like '95, though, these wines are worth exploring, particularly in this hyperinflated market. But caution is indicated. Tasting through a selection of the '95 second labels, I was sometimes disappointed. Ideally, we're talking about the difference between Armani's black label and its less expensive white label, but often these second wines are the equivalent of no-name knockoffs.

The best place to choose a second wine is at the address of a *grand vin* that you admire. Haut-Brion is perhaps my favorite first growth, and I've found the lesser Bahans Haut-Brion to share some of the smoky, earthy characteristics of the great wine that enchanted diarist Samuel Pepys. In a year like '89 it is the match of many classed growths. Cheval Blanc, long considered a first growth, despite the oversight of the 1855 committee, also bottles Le Petit Cheval, although you may have to wait for your next trip to France to score a bottle. Lafleur, which some consider the equal of its neighbor Pétrus, makes one of the rarest and greatest second wines, Les Pensées de Lafleur. If you ever see a bottle, call me.

Two of the most consistently excellent second labels come from Léoville Las Cases and Lynch-Bages. The former château, a second growth, introduced its second label, Clos du Marquis, in 1904. The '95 is the best second-label wine that I've tasted, sensationally rich and long of finish. Lynch-Bages, nominally a fifth growth, is near the top of everyone's list of great châteaux, and their second label, Haut-Bages-Avérous, is always worth seeking out. Others to look for, in no particular order: Réserve de la Comtesse (Pichon-Longueville—Comtesse de Lalande), La Dame de Montrose (Montrose), Ségla (Rausan-Ségla), and Les Fiefs de Lagrange (Lagrange). Most of these wines are ready to drink upon release, unlike their big brothers and sisters. Which is reason enough to check them out, even if, by the time you read this, disaster in the international financial markets has tempered the price of the *grands vins*.

SAINT-EMILION GETS SEXY

You don't meet too many winemakers who identify themselves as Aristotelians. But then you don't meet too many winemakers like François Mitjavile of Le Tertre Roteboeuf. Shifting his weight from one ragged blue espadrille to the other on the cold floor of his cellar, he looks like a youngish Joseph Heller, with wiry salt-and-pepper hair and a bemused grin. For the past four years Mitjavile has been retracing the history of philosophy, starting with Heraclitus. "I don't like Plato," he says. "Or Descartes. There is no one truth. There is variety. This is why I like Aristotle." This soliloquy comes in response to a French critic who complained that Mitjavile's '89 Tertre Roteboeuf—which we are drinking—was too decadent and ripe to be a "classic"; though Mitjavile's rejection of Platonic absolutes might apply just as well to Robert Parker's hundred-point rating scale, on which the '89 Tertre Roteboeuf scored a whopping ninety-four points. "We are not objective creatures," Mitjavile says. "Is Mozart better than Beethoven? We never love things absolutely. We love them through our emotions. The idea is not to make the best wine. The idea is to make a wine that is the expression of the locale and the soil."

Improbably named "the hill of the belching beef," Mitjavile's locale is a beautiful amphitheater-shaped vineyard that unscrolls from an absurdly picturesque eighteenth-century church not far from the medieval village of Saint-Émilion. When I visited him on the first of October, 1997, the grapes were still hanging on the vines. Most of his neighbors had picked theirs already, but Mitjavile was waiting, despite the nervousness of his distributor, former rugby star Dominique Renard, who wandered the vineyard with brow furrowed, noting that some of the grapes were already raisiny. Mitjavile retorted that the bulk of them had yet to reach optimum ripeness.

Year in and year out, Mitjavile risks late-season rain and frost to produce one of the richest, most characterful wines in all of Bordeaux. Unfortunately, he makes only two thousand cases a year, not many of which will make it to the States. Fortunately, Saint-Émilion has many dedicated small producers who are turning out wines that can rival those made at the famous châteaux of the Médoc, an hour and a half to the west. In fact, Saint-Émilion is the largest red-wine appellation of Bordeaux. As opposed to Pauillac, which resembles

Iowa speckled with enormous Beaux Arts châteaux, it *looks* like great wine country—a picturesque region of small growers such as Mitjavile who tend to consider themselves farmers rather than chatelains. It has also become the hottest appellation in Bordeaux, with new small-production wines like Valandraud and La Mondotte selling for absurd, Pétrus-like prices.

One of the virtues of the wines of Saint-Émilion is that with their high percentage of Merlot—as much as 90 percent—they are usually flirtier than their Cabernet-based Left Bank cousins and are approachable at an earlier age. Merlot can be a wimpy, insipid grape in warmer regions, but the climate and soil of Saint-Émilion and neighboring Pomerol seem to be its natural habitat. The locals, still annoyed that they were left out of the famous classification of 1855, developed their own classification, which is no more reliable than its predecessor except that it can supposedly be revised every ten years. (The 1996 revision, however, was absurdly inadequate.) In descending order the levels are Premier Grand Cru Classé, Grand Cru Classé, and Grand Cru. (Excuse me—the lowest category is Grand Cru? Madison Avenue's got nothing on these farmers.) Alone among the thirteen Premier Grand Cru Classés, Cheval Blanc and Ausone are considered by connoisseurs to be first growths on a par with Margaux and Latour. Personally, I think the austere Ausone is best suited to very rich ascetics with very long life expectancies. The velvety, luxurious Cheval Blanc is the equal of any wine in Bordeaux, and I wish I could afford it on some kind of regular basis. The '95 is fantastic—one more reason to hate the rich.

The demotic excitement in Saint-Émilion comes from wines like L'Arrosée—one of my favorites—which is usually an exotic, voluptuous treat; and Monbousquet, which has suddenly emerged from the pack as a serious wine and, unlike the increasingly spectacular L'Angélus, is still affordable for those of us who fly commercial. Troplong-Mondot, Canon La Gaffelière, and Magdelaine are among the rising stars of the appellation. The fastidious François Mitjavile recommends Dassault, Barde-Haut, and Beauséjour-Bécot— apparently favoring the early part of the alphabet. Another *B* to watch for is Belair, where Pascal Delbeck, Ausone's former cellar master, is in residence. Dominique Renard advises thrifty oenophiles to watch for Lucie, Vieux Fortin, Ferrand-Lartigue, and Bellefont-Belcier. Every vintage seems to produce a new crop of so-called *vins de garage*—boutique wines made in tiny quantities on the model of Valandraud.

Just when it seems that Saint-Émilion can't get any hotter, along comes the '98 vintage. Unlike the Left Bank of Pauillac and Saint-Julien, Saint-Émilion experienced a near-perfect growing season. Unfortunately, the rising quality is reflected in the prices. Consider cutting back on food, clothing, and taxis so as to be able to stock up on the '98s. That's me on the subway, wearing *last year's* Prada suit, reading Aristotle while I wait for my few bottles of the '98 Tertre Roeboeuf to mature.

CHIANTI COMEBACK

Rather like pop star George Michael, Chianti has had a confusing image over the past couple of decades. Is it thin, bouncy background music to food, à la Wham!, or is it the sultry "I Want Your Sex" world-beat potion that has begun to appear under certain labels in the past decade? Is it a pure expression of the Sangiovese grape? Or is it a Sangiovese-based blend of grapes meant to express the Tuscan terrain?

So renowned were the wines of the Chianti hills between Florence and Siena that in 1726 the Grand Duke of Tuscany, Cosimo the Third, decided to issue a proclamation restricting the use of the name and setting geographical boundaries, thus creating Italy's first officially designated wine region. By the 1960s, though, the name *Chianti* had become more or less synonymous with *plonk*.

Certainly the Chianti of our youth was a simple beverage, notably mainly for the squat, straw-wrapped bottle that was the candlestick and bong component of choice in dorm rooms around the world. The tomato sauce that Chianti inevitably accompanied pretty much canceled out the nasty acidity—and most of the faint fruit as well. By 1967, when government (DOC) regulations codified winemaking practices and geographic boundaries of the wines of Chianti (and the more exclusive Chianti Classico), standards were so low that certain of the region's growers chose to opt out of the Consortium of Chianti Classico Producers and even to drop the name *Chianti* from their wines altogether. In addition to allowing incredibly high yields, the DOC regulations at that time called for all wines bearing the Chianti name to include at least 10 percent of the white grapes Trebbiano and Malvasia. Whatever the historical reasons for this practice, it made Chianti wimpier and less age-worthy than it might have been.

When the more ambitious Chianti producers turned their backs on the name in the 1970s, the so-called Super Tuscan movement was born: Makers like Antinori, Fonterutoli, and Montevertine threw out the rule book to create premium wines that could compete in the international marketplace. Some used nontraditional grapes like Cabernet Sauvignon, and some sought a higher expression of the native Sangiovese, the primary grape in the Chianti recipe. A rivalry began to take shape as wealthy émigrés from other parts of Italy bought up derelict properties in the region. Sergio Manetti, a wealthy manufacturer, bought the rundown Montevertine estate to run as a hobby in 1967, and within a decade was creating one of the great wines of Tuscany, blissfully ignoring the DOC regulations. Lombardian Fabrizio Bianchi, whose family bought the ancient Monsanto estate in 1961, likewise found himself at odds with the old rules.

If he was not born here, Bianchi takes his steward-ship of the rugged, deeply folded land with the passion of a convert, as does his daughter Laura, who will in-herit this venerable domain and who already knows every inch of it. Watching Laura walk the rows of the Monsanto vineyards explaining why they are "the best in Chianti"—a claim one hears from *all* growers in Chianti—it's not hard to imagine this former law stu-dent cruising Via Montenapoleone on her way to the Valentino boutique, or strutting down the runway modeling resortwear, though she insists she's a country girl. Despite the emphasis on the importance of the land, the Bianchis, like many of the new wave of Tuscan winemakers, have embraced the latest wine-making technology—their new cellars are full of computer-monitored stainless-steel fermenting tanks and new French oak *barriques.*

Fabrizio Bianchi has always believed in the age-worthiness of Sangiovese-based wines. In 1968 he stopped using white grapes in his Chianti Classico, a radical move that put him at odds with the Consortium of Chianti Classico Producers. In 1974 he bottled a 100 percent Sangiovese wine, which he named for himself, one of the first of what would eventually be called Super Tuscan reds. That same year marked the release of Antinori's Tignanello, which blended small amounts of Cabernet with the native Sangiovese; Sassicaia, a powerful 100 percent Cabernet Sauvignon, which is grown to the east of the Chianti region, on the Tuscan coast; and Le Pergole Torte, a Sangiovese from the Montevertine estate in Chianti Classico. Since none of these wines fits the restrictions of the Chianti Classico regulations, they were classified as *vini da tavola*—the most humble category in the Italian system. And yet many of these wines were soon more renowned than the official Chiantis. Now every grower you visit in Chianti will tell you without fail that he made the very first Super Tuscan wine.

Bianchi, who bottles Chianti Classicos as well as Super Tuscans, maintains a library of several thousand bottles of each vintage in his cellars in order to test the evolution of the wines, and he frequently re-releases older vintages to the market. At a late-summer lunch at the family's villa, cooked by Fabrizio's wife, Giuliana, I was amazed by the quality of the older vintages. Given the regulations and the casual winemaking practices of the past, the real capabilities of Sangiovese are only beginning to be understood, but if the '75 Fabrizio Bianchi that I tasted is any indication, the potential is significant. Bianchi is a fan of Burgundy, and his '75 tasted like nothing so much as an aged Gevrey-Chambertin. Like Pinot Noir, Sangiovese is evocative of cherries in its youth and mushrooms in its maturity; it's more of a lover than a fighter, lighter in color than Cabernet or Syrah. His 100 percent Cabernet Nemo proves that point, but Bianchi's true love is Sangiovese. "It's more difficult, but finally more elegant," he says. His flagship Chianti Classico, called Il Poggio, is made from 90 percent Sangiovese, with smaller amounts of the traditional Canaiolo and Colorino. The '69, which we tasted at lunch, is still giving pleasure with tastes of licorice and cedar. Granted, I may have been influenced by Fabrizio's feisty and erudite commentary, or by the quieter charms of Laura Bianchi, or by the view of the steep Tuscan hills rising beyond the windows of the dining room. But subsequent tasting of the newer vintages suggests that their wines, like those of many of their neighbors in Chianti, are getting better all the time.

The aristocratic and photogenic Mazzei family, which has owned the same Chianti Classico estate, Castello di Fonterutoli, since 1435, was among those who broke ranks with the Consortium of Chianti Classico Producers by creating the Super Tuscan called Concerto in 1981. With the '95 vintage, the family decided to return to its roots and focus its energies on making Chianti Classico. (Classico is the region referred to in the Grand Duke's original proclamation, as opposed to the much larger area since designated Chianti.) In recent years the Consortium of Chianti Classico, whose wine bottles wear a band with a black rooster label around their necks, has revised its regulations to allow more flexibility for ambitious producers like Fonterutoli. "We experimented for a while," says Francesco Mazzei, stooping to examine wild boar tracks at the edge of a Cabernet vineyard. "It was a great thing. Now the idea is to make a Super Chianti Classico."

Among those who have kept the faith, even through the dark ages of the 1950s and 1960s, is the Stucchi Prinetti family, owners of Badia a Coltibuono, probably the most famous estate in Chianti. The high visibility of the estate, and of Chianti itself, owes much to the charismatic and cosmopolitan Emanuela Stucchi Prinetti—who would be played by Anne Archer or Isabella Rossellini in *Chianti: The Movie*—while the improved quality of Badia wine is the work of her brother Roberto, who studied winemaking in California and still has the ponytail and laid-back demeanor of a Berkeley hippie. The eleventh-century monastery that the family inhabits also houses stocks of ancient vintages. The wine is now made in a stunning new Piero Sartogo–designed winery, which manages to seem monumental and modest at the same time, set against a hillside near the town of Monti. Another striking visual symbol of the innovation/tradition dialectic in Chianti is at the hilltop estate of Castello di Volpaia, where huge, shiny stainless-steel fermenting tanks reach nearly to the ceiling of a deconsecrated thirteenth-century church. Volpaia turns out consistently strong Chianti Classicos.

While many of the old estates have undergone a re-birth, newcomers and small growers are also part of the Chianti renaissance. One of the best is Casaloste, which offered its first vintage in '93. Giovanni Battista d'Orsi and his wife, Emilia, are refugees from Naples, where he studied agronomy and oenology. Their mod-est ranch home sits in the middle of a seventeen-acre vineyard. The barrel-chested, goateed Giovanni grows the grapes organically and makes the wine, while ex-banker Emilia, looking very retro in cat's-eye glasses, helps with sales. Their Chianti Classicos are stunning and, at around twenty dollars, a good value. The d'Orsis chose to join the consortium, which now spon-sors extensive research into Sangiovese clones, soil types, and vinification, in addition to promoting wines.

Chianti Classico comes in two grades: regular and riserva. The former is a younger, simpler wine, usually aged and released within a year of harvest. These wines are often very good values, particularly in strong years like '95 and '96, and especially in a spectacular year like '97. Chianti Classico Riserva is made from grapes ripe enough to attain at least 12.5 percent alcohol and is aged for a minimum of twenty-seven months. These wines are richer, fuller, and more age-worthy. Current regulations allow the addition of up to 15 percent Cabernet or other red-wine grapes, but Chianti re-mains based on Sangiovese, which seems to do better in the Tuscan hills than anywhere else in the world. "There are some grapes that carry their passports in their pockets and can travel all over the world," says

Giovanni Manetti, the handsome son of the proprietor of the renowned Fontodi estate. "They can go anywhere. But Sangiovese is local." Sangiovese doesn't have the brute strength of Cabernet or the voluptuousness of Merlot, but new vinification techniques have tamed the astringency and acidity of the old straw-bottled stuff. Like burgundy, Chianti complements a far greater range of food than most wines made from those two slightly arrogant and cosmopolitan grapes.

SLOW-MO MONTALCINO
BRUNELLO DI MONTALCINO

"Barolo is the Bach of wine . . . strong, supremely structured, a little forbidding, but absolutely fundamental. Barbaresco is the Beethoven, taking those qualities and lifting them to heights of subjective passion and pain . . . and Brunello is its Brahms, the softer, fuller, romantic afterglow of so much strenuous excess."
—Michael Dibdin, *A Long Finish*

Perched at the peak of a steep, forbidding hill surmounted by a medieval fortress, the town of Montalcino towers over the surrounding countryside. The same landscape that proved so forbidding to centuries of would-be invaders has resulted in a certain cultural isolation. In the 1970s and 1980s, the red wine known as

Brunello di Montalcino achieved international renown, but recently its reputation has lagged somewhat in relation to other areas of Tuscany. While the Antinori family and a slew of wealthy Milanese carpetbaggers were reviving the fortunes of Chianti and creating new stars like Sassicaia and Ornellaia in Bolgheri, the sometimes stubborn and long-lived Brunellos have come to seem a little dowdy. Change has come slowly to this part of Tuscany. These earthy, masculine wines require patience and, perhaps, a champion.

For better *and* for worse, the fortunes of Brunello di Montalcino are inextricably linked with the Biondi-Santi family. The wine was created in the 1880s by Ferruccio Biondi-Santi, scion of a landowning family who had fought with Garibaldi's forces at the Battle of Bezzecca. At the family's estate, Il Greppo, Ferruccio isolated a local clone of the Sangiovese grape called Sangiovese Grosso that yielded large clusters of grapes, described as *brunello* because of the darkness of the skin when ripe. At the time the region was best known for sweet whites made from the Moscadello grape; the local reds were light, spritzy beverages that weren't meant to last beyond the succeeding vintage. When he took over Il Greppo, Ferruccio decided to create a new style of full-bodied red wine aged in wood casks.

As Ferruccio's wines began to command attention, and high prices, his neighbors began to imitate his practices. When Italy first codified regional winemaking practices in 1963, the laws governing Brunello di

Montalcino followed. The new laws, which followed Biondi-Santi's practices, were among the most restrictive in Italy, requiring four years of aging before release (five years for the riservas). The naturally high acidity of the Sangiovese Grosso grape makes further aging almost imperative, unless you plan to dump it in your car battery. The glory of Brunello is that it continues to improve and develop complexity for years; Ferruccio's 1888 vintage has continued to astound those lucky enough to have tasted it in recent decades. (The 1955 is legendary, earning a spot on the *Wine Spectator's* list of ten wines of the century. I can personally confirm that the 1964 is also sensational, and still developing.)

Ferrucio's grandson Franco presides over Il Greppo. A slim, elegant aristocrat who was wearing a beautiful single-breasted khaki suit with a crisp blue oxford shirt and tie when I met him at his villa one hot summer day in 1997, he is not a man who believes in instant gratification, or in change for its own sake. (Or, some would say, for any other sake.) There is no stainless steel or new oak in the cellar at Il Greppo. "I don't trust the new technology," he says. "I don't know what it will yield in thirty years." He is as proud of the old cement fermentation tanks as he is of the vast library of dusty old bottles dating back to the previous century, and he is frugal enough to return the leftover wine in our tasting glasses from the old chestnut barrels it has just been drawn from. He also proud of his north-facing-vineyards, which further accentuate the high acidity of the Sangiovese; while he doesn't name any names, he dismisses the potential of the vineyards on the south side of Montalcino.

Angelo Gaja is the new kid in town, having purchased, some five years ago, a vineyard on—you guessed it—the south side of town. Gaja is the man who made Barbaresco famous, the hyperactive perfectionist who introduced new French oak *barriques* to Italian grapes (not to mention sticker shock to those who thought of Italian wines as cheap). And he may be the man who helps bring Brunello di Montalcino into the new millennium. Gaja chose the estate of Pieve Santa Restituta in part because of his admiration for the wines of the neighboring Casse Basse estate. Gianfranco Soldera of Casse Basse is another carpetbagger, a maverick from Milan who produces tiny amounts of rich, expensive, and relatively voluptuous Brunello. (Despite his feud with the editors of *Gambero Rosso*, the bible of the Italian wine world, his juice is coveted in Italy; few cases make it beyond his native Milan.)

Gaja's '95 Brunellos—the first great vintage over which he had full control—will almost certainly create new admirers for the region even as its super-ripe, heavily oaked style will annoy traditionalists like Biondi-Santi. If Gaja's Barbarescos are any indication, these wines will develop for years but will be drinkable far sooner than Biondi-Santi's, whose '95 vintage should be coming around about the time my five-year-old twins start collecting Social Security. As austere as

Gaja's young wines can seem, they are positively voluptuous by comparison.

Another recent arrival, the artist Sandro Chia, is helping define the evolving style of Brunello. When he bought the derelict medieval fortress of Castello Rumitorio, Chia decided to cultivate some of the prime vineyard land that came with it. "The locals thought I was crazy spending what I did on my vineyards," Chia says, reflecting the fact that for all of Montalcino's fame, this is still largely a region of small farmer and growers. "I went to the local wine store with a friend and listened as the store owner described the crazy artist on the hill and his lavish ways with money." Chia's first vintages, produced by former Biondi-Santi employee Carlo Vittori, are extremely promising—the old-style Brunello power finessed by the practical magic of new technology.

Recently it's become fashionable in the wine press to complain about the prices of Brunello (fifty dollars and up for regular bottlings, released after four years, and approximately seventy-five dollars and up for the riservas, which are released after five years). Brunello has always been expensive partly because it has a proven ability to evolve and improve over time—something that cannot be said of some of the new Super Tuscans or California Cabernets, which sell for upward of a hundred dollars a bottle. Unfortunately, many of these wines are consumed in restaurants shortly after release. This is called infanticide. It's not against the law yet, but it should be. A good Brunello, including those from the new high-tech voluptuaries like Gaja and Chia, should never be consumed before its tenth birthday. If you want instant gratification, try Rosso di Montalcino, a far more affordable version (fifteen to thirty-five dollars) that's released sooner and generally ready to drink upon release.

This is a great moment to discover the wines of Montalcino. The '95 Brunellos—the first great vintage since '90—were released in the spring of 2000. And while you wait for the spectacular '97 Brunellos, drink the '97 and '98 Rossos. Or try to lay your hands on some older Brunellos. As a rule of thumb, they mature at about the same rate we do.

THE SWEET THEREAFTER

THE CLOSER
SAUTERNES

The only problem with so-called dessert wines, in my opinion, is dessert. Hemingway is supposed to have said that any man who eats dessert is not drinking enough. Certainly, if you're drinking wine with your dinner, you're already getting plenty of sugar. And if you're lucky enough to have a bottle of Sauternes with which to finish the meal, dessert seems doubly redundant. Although I'm a fan of the sweet wines of Germany, the Loire, and Alsace, it's hard to argue with the supremacy of Sauternes (and its neighbor Barsac). The fact is, most Sauternes are too damn good to sing backup to some creamy, sugary solid.

Decadently rich, sweet, sticky, and expensive, Sauternes may be the perfect fin de siècle wine, the counterpart of the prose of Walter Pater or the poetry of Verlaine. The *Fleurs du Mal* soul of Sauternes is a fungus called *Botrytis cinerea*. There are many ways to make sweet wine, but none of them can reproduce the rich flavor of the "noble rot" that infects ripening grapes in the cooling vineyards of Sauternes and Barsac during the fall months, when the mists from the Garonne River set in. Not since Baudelaire smoked opium has corruption resulted in such beauty. Initially, though, it's not a pretty picture. The late Hugh Johnson describes the botrytized fruit: "A heavy web of greenish grey mold, with short hairs growing outwards, covers the grapes; each grape has partially or totally collapsed, and, if handled, readily exudes sticky juice and a cloud of mold spores." Miraculously, the wine from these funky, blackened grapes eventually emerges clear and golden colored from the barrel. The botrytis also stimulates the production of glycerol, which gives a good Sauternes its thick, viscous texture.

If all the grapes rotted on the same day at the same rate, life would be considerably easier for the Sauternians, and Sauternes would be far cheaper for the rest of us. Even in the best years, though, the grapes rot unevenly, requiring multiple passes through the vineyards by the pickers, who, at the best châteaux, select individual grapes rather than bunches. This process is expensive; furthermore, the shriveled grapes yield less juice per acre than their healthy counterparts, as little as half to a quarter of the red-grape yields in the Médoc. All of which make Sauternes expensive to produce. And to buy. Given the difficulties of production, good Sauternes is a great value.

In some years botrytis fails to set in at all, which is why vintage quality may not correlate with that of other regions of Bordeaux. For Bordeaux reds and dry whites, '85 was a terrific year, but the near-failure of botrytis makes it a mediocre year, at best, for Sauternes. Sauternes and Barsac had a string of good to great years in the 1980s: Look for '81, '83, '86, '88, and '89. The last year is especially recommended, being not only great but still somewhat available, and, except for Yquem, approaching maturity. The '90 is also superb but was released at much higher prices in the United States than the '89 vintage. If you're looking for some sweet stuff to lay down, go for the '95s and the '97s.

The apotheosis of Sauternes, in terms of both price and excellence, is Château d'Yquem. In no other wine region of the world is the superiority of one property so universally acknowledged. All you have to do is taste a mature example to understand why. I didn't even blink recently when a friend who is far more knowledgeable about wine than I am said that it's his favorite wine in the world. The proprietors of Yquem have often said that an entire vine yields but a single glass of this ambrosia, and few who have experienced the concentration would doubt it. Yquem is capable of aging and improving for fifty years or longer, losing some of its honeyed sweetness as it gains in complexity. My own greatest-hits list would include the '55, '59, and '67. The wine costs far more than other Sauternes, and it's unquestionably worth it. I'm not sure that Dom Pérignon is three times as good as Moët, but I will swear that Yquem is three times better than, say, Rieussec. If drinking Sauternes in general is a little like reading Walter Pater on Leonardo da Vinci, drinking Yquem is like *being* Leonardo.

Yquem's excellent sister château, de Fargues, is more affordable and clearly related to its sibling. Among the other great properties are Climens, Rieussec, Raymond-Lafon, Sudiuraut, Guiraud, Coutet, and Gillette. Those who have missed out on the current stock-market boom might consider the sweet wines of nearby Monbazillac—the workingman's Sauternes. These wines are often nearly as good as some of the classified Sauternes; many can be purchased in this country for less than thirty dollars, and they are often more food-friendly, being somewhat lighter in body.

Speaking of foods, if we must, there are some that go beautifully with Sauternes—though they are not necessarily desserts. The sweetness of Sauternes makes it a good match for salty foods, like Roquefort. Ham and Sauternes is excellent; ditto prosciutto and melon, either together or separately. Anytime you can eat foie gras with Yquem it's easily worth the three-week loss of life expectancy. But beware—this combo is hard to follow; don't open a '55 Mouton after a '55 Yquem with foie gras, as a generous host once did for me. The Mouton might as well have been Beaujolais.

PORT WITHOUT PURDAH

Like the English novel, vintage port seemed destined for extinction after the Second World War. In fact, it was hard to imagine the former without the latter— Fieldingesque, fox-hunting squires in their drafty dining halls getting stupider on the stuff, all those literary, country-house dinner parties ending with drawing room purdah for the women, cigars and port in the library for the men. Happily, Brit lit and vintage port are thriving again, and the enjoyment of port no longer entails forgoing the company of the opposite sex. The annoying new popularity of cigars in this country can only increase the interest in this sublime after-dinner diversion.

Though it hails from Portugal, port as we know it was invented by swashbuckling English wine shippers who were forced to look beyond Bordeaux during the late-seventeenth-century trade wars between England and France. Legend has it that the wines they discovered in the hot, arid Douro Valley were first fortified with one-quarter part brandy in order to preserve them on the long, hot ocean voyage to the north. Adding the brandy during fermentation, before the grape sugar had fully converted to alcohol, left residual sugar, resulting in the sweet red wine we know today.

The added brandy contributes to port's incredible longevity—good ports from major years can easily improve for fifty years and last for a hundred; I recently enjoyed a lovely 1908 Cockburn in London. (Actually, the label had fallen off long ago—Sotheby's had thoughtfully affixed a new label, which read, "1908 presumed Cockburn.") On the downside, the brandy and the residual sugar contribute mightily to your hangover. Not to mention the fact that you have inevitably thrown back a few glasses of the dry red stuff and perhaps the odd cocktail before you get to the port. The alcohol level of most ports is around 20 percent— as opposed to a rough average of 12 percent for dry red wines—but the next day you may have a hard time believing that it's not even higher. This may be the place to say that it's never a good idea to pour a third glass of port, no matter how excellent the plan seems at the time. And even the second should not be undertaken lightly, particularly by those who hope to get lucky, or to drive home, like patriotic Americans, on the right-hand side of the road.

I was recently asked what a good port should taste like. The obvious answer is that nothing else tastes like a great vintage port. As with all great wines, each year and maker possesses its unique nuances. But on reflection, I am willing to propose a kind of faux port experience for the uninitiated. Take a Smith Brothers sour cherry cough drop and affix it to a Callard & Bowser butterscotch with melted Godiva dark chocolate. Insert in mouth. Suck. On the other hand, there's also a good case to be made for the Raisinets analogy.

What goes with port? The classic British accompaniment of Stilton is hard to argue with, unless you don't like Stilton. Despite the English tradition of dry red wine and cheese, port is one of the few reds that will stand up to big, aged cheeses. Port can be the perfect accompaniment to chocolate. Figs are also a classic accompaniment. However, when faced with a brilliant and mature vintage port, it's probably best to treat it as a dessert in itself. It's not as if you're not going to get your sugar fix.

Some of the encrusted rituals of port drinking, like sexual segregation and passing it to the left, are strictly optional. However, decanting is a pretty good idea. Vintage ports throw off a lot of sediment, which can be disturbed in pouring, and which will definitely foul your wine if it ends up in the glass. Port should be stored on its side and stood upright a day before pouring. Decant slowly. Cheesecloth or a swatch of discarded panty hose can help catch the sediment. A common misconception: Port will keep indefinitely in a stoppered decanter. Younger vintage ports with lots of stuffing will last longer than unfortified wines, but seldom more than a few days after opening.

Ninety-eight percent of port production goes into relatively inexpensive, undated wine. Vintage port is bottled only in those years that are judged to be superior by the individual houses. Sometimes there is a general agreement about the year. The great years of recent times are '63, '70, '77, '83, and '85. Some houses declared '91 a vintage year, others '92. The '94s are already legendary, though they are at least a decade away from any kind of drinkability. I keep kicking myself for failing to buy a case for my son, who was born that year; the prices having doubled and tripled since release, with the Taylor and Fonseca trading north of $150 a bottle. The '97 also appears to be a great vintage.

For a variety of reasons, including the collapse of the London port market during the British recession in the early 1990s, port prices for certain recent vintages have remained moderate in comparison with Bordeaux prices. The magnificent '63s are now heady **in price,** though still reasonable compared to the '61 Bordeaux; the '77s, which generally still need time, are surpassing a hundred dollars a bottle. The wise buyer, it seems to me, would stock up on '77 or the great, undervalued '85 vintage, which is approaching drinkability even as it promises to last well into the millennium. Prices for most '85s remain close to the prices at which they were released, in distinction to, say, the '85 Bordeaux, which have more or less quadrupled. And they are in some cases less expensive than the '94s, which won't be fit to drink until the Red Sox win the World Series or my children graduate from college, whichever comes second.

SWEET STUFF FROM ITALY
VINI DOLCI

If one were to find a fault with any aspect of Italian cuisine—aside from the fact that the term itself is a something of a convenient fiction, referring to dozens of diverse regional cuisines—it would be with the paucity of memorable desserts. Tira misu, pannacotta, gelato . . . that's about all that leaps to mind for me. Fortunately, this third-act weakness at the Italian table is more than compensated for by the abundance of delicious sweet wines, or *vini dolci*, which, to my mind, make a better and more stimulating conclusion to a meal than any of the above.

Probably the best-known Italian sweet wine is Vin Santo, aka "Holy Wine," which hails from Tuscany and is traditionally made from Trebbiano and Malvasia grapes that have been dried on straw mats under the rafters of the attic, a process that concentrates the grape sugars. In his book *A Tuscan in the Kitchen,* restaurateur Pino Longo suggests an explanation for the righteous name: "When I was a kid, my father told me the monks used to travel from door to door throughout Tuscany to bring charitable assistance to the sick and the elderly, always offering a shot of this mysterious sweet wine. Since it had the power to give a little relief from suffering and loneliness, the wine became known among the peasants as Vin Santo." An alternate explanation I heard in Chianti is that the wine is considered holy because a significant amount of the stuff is shared with the angels while it is aging—and evaporating—in small oak and chestnut casks.

Holy it may be, but the quality of Vin Santo varies wildly, some of it tasting every bit as bad as the altar wine I used to sample when I was an altar boy. The level of residual sugar—and sweetness—varies wildly as well. Some of the drier Vin Santos taste very much like dry sherry. Not necessarily a compliment in my book. Being aged in heated attics often results in maderization (i.e., heat damage). The best Vin Santos can be fascinating. The worst can make you incredibly grateful for the biscotti with which they are inevitably served. (They are supposed to be dunked in the holy beverage.)

Italy's other great red-wine region, the Piedmont, produces a number of delicious sweet whites. Like the food of this beautiful, mountainous area, these still tend to be underappreciated in this country. Perhaps the most refreshing is Moscato d'Asti, a very light, slightly fizzy expression of Muscat, Piedmont's oldest varietal and the world's most versatile dessert-wine grape. It may be necessary to block out your associations with brash Asti Spumante in order to appreciate the virtues of its near-relative. If Asti is basically Jerry Springer, Moscato d'Asti is more like Dennis Miller. A good Moscato d'Asti is like a spritzy liquid sorbet and has the virtue of being very light in alcohol—as low as 5 percent. (If this seems like a drawback, you can always have a second glass.) Richer, nonfizzy styles of Muscat are also made in the Piedmont, and some of these can be very serious. The quality of these seems to me consistently higher than with Vin Santo.

The most promising area for white-wine production, both sweet and dry, is the northeast—the back thigh of Italy, as it were, from Verona up to the Austrian border. Friuli, source of some of Italy's best dry whites, also produces several interesting sweet wines, like Picolit. Made from the grape of the same name, Picolit was a favorite of some of the most epicurean European courts of the eighteenth century. Like many Italian dessert wines, this one is produced by the Recioto or "raisining" method, the grape bunches being dried out on mats before pressing. Some estates harvest very late to maximize sweetness. Either way they get hefty prices for this delicate nectar, which is much prized by the Italians themselves.

Nearby Soave, which produced so much of the insipid white liquid we sloshed down while listening to

Cat Stevens and Dan Fogelberg, is enjoying a renaissance. Among the makers of wonderful dessert-style Soaves are Anselmi, Sandro and Claudino Gini, La Cappucina, and Umberto Portinari. Valpolicella is another incredibly lame wine of the Veneto that is threatening to become worthwhile. Receito della Valpolicella is a sweet red, of all things, produced by the raisining method. Look for those made by Tedeschi and Tommaso Bussola. It's an excellent novelty at the dinner table and a good accompaniment to light chocolate dishes.

Although the north of Italy produces far greater wines at the moment, the future probably lies to the south. Among the signs of Sicily's great potential are the sweet and velvety Moscatos of the Pantelleria region, such as those from Salvatore Murana and D'Ancona.

As far as I can tell, Italy produces more varieties of *vino dolci* than France does cheese—a situation that is both inspiring and daunting. Among my New Year's resolutions: to devote part of the new millennium to exploring their variety in situ as well as in my favorite New York trattorias. All of those who made unlikely vows about calories this year should remember that unlike Pastry, pudding, and cake, a glass of *vino dolci* is super-low in fat and cholesterol.

GRAPE NUTS

THE BIGGEST
CRITIC IN THE
WORLD

On the day Robert M. Parker Jr. left Manhattan's Restaurant Daniel on a stretcher, his main concern, aside from the fact that he might be having a coronary, was that he would be missing out on the magnum of '47 Château Cheval Blanc on his table. Despite such worries, and a certain amount of physical discomfort, he was able to summon enough wit to tell New York governor George Pataki, who was just entering the restaurant as Parker was carried past, "Don't eat the scallops." (Parker's ailment turned out to be fairly minor and unrelated to his meal.) This was probably the first time that a wine critic made the *New York Post*'s Page Six. But in the wine world, Parker has been the boldest of bold-faced names for the past fifteen years, the Michael Jordan of wine tasting.

If anyone needs verification of Parker's nonpareil stature, it was recently provided by, of all people, the French. The self-proclaimed American Wine Advocate, who at the start of his career couldn't even speak the language, was recently awarded the Légion d'Honneur for telling the Frogs that a lot of their venerable Bordeaux and Burgundy isn't as great as it should be and that some of it positively sucks. The *French!* He's saying this, not about their mothers or their girlfriends, but about their *wine!* And last June Chirac kissed both of his cheeks and gave him one of those goddamn little medals to wear on his lapel for the rest of his life! *Incroyable!* Even Parker himself was blown away—he proudly displayed snapshots at a recent lunch—and believe me, he is not a guy who lacks self-confidence.

The first issue of Parker's *The Wine Advocate* (then called *The Baltimore-Washington Wine Advocate*) appeared in 1978. The nine-page newsletter opened with a survey of the '73 Bordeaux vintage, which had already been touted by the trade. Parker informed his handful of readers that "with a few exceptions, the wines are disappointing and overpriced relative to quality." Wines were graded on the good old American hundred-point report-card scale. Châteaux Margaux, the famous first growth, received a failing grade of fifty-five points. "A poorly made wine that should be avoided," the report concluded. If anyone in the insular wine world had noticed, they might have said, "Who the hell does this guy think he is?" At the time

Parker was a moonlighting corporate lawyer publishing the newsletter out of his home in rural Maryland.

Parker knew nothing about wine in 1967, when he first visited France as a college student to rendezvous with his high school sweetheart, Pat Etzel. As an impoverished traveler, he discovered that wine was the cheapest beverage on most menus. By the time he returned to the States, an obsession had been born. After graduation he went to law school, he says, "because I didn't want to go to work." He married Pat, who looks remarkably like the young Natalie Wood in their honeymoon pictures and who served as his translator on their increasingly frequent visits to the vineyards of France. (Parker has since learned to speak French and insists on using it out of respect for his hosts.)

As his avocation became a vocation, Parker quit practicing law and became the most respected, admired, and feared wine critic in the world, educating a generation of American consumers—myself included—and influencing the way that wine is made and sold around the world. A single point on his rating scale can be worth hundreds of thousands of dollars to a winemaker. His books, which include *Bordeaux, Burgundy,* and *Wines of the Rhône Valley,* are published in more than half a dozen languages, including French. Such is his perceived importance that he has received death threats (later traced to a retailer formerly based in Manhattan) and was sued for libel by a French wine *négotiant.* He is mobbed by women when he visits Japan. He recently turned down a *60 Minutes* profile. And did I mention the Légion d'Honneur?

I first met Parker at a charity dinner at which he was the guest of honor. The dinner included tasting of the first growths of Bordeaux; the owners of the great estates were there, and I was amazed at the incredible deference these French potentates paid to Parker. He might have been Nelson Mandela . . . or Jerry Lewis. Also impressive was his almost childlike enthusiasm for the wine. "After a quarter of a million wines that have run across my palate," he declared, "I still get excited by wines like these."

"I'm a hedonist," he told me a few months later at a restaurant near his home, to which he had generously carried a bottle of '95 Domaine Michel Niellon Chassagne-Montrachet and an '88 Château Rayas from one of his three cellars. "My hobbies are wine and food. People keep asking me when I'm going to lose a few pounds, and I say, 'It took millions of dollars to get into this shape.' " While he is far thinner and more handsome than, say, A. J. Liebling, one feels for those stretcher bearers at Daniel. Parker is a big man in every sense. His prose, too, is robust and muscular—hardly the norm for wine writing. He tells me about a ten-course tasting menu at Charlie Trotter's in Chicago that left him unsatisfied: "Afterward we went to a place called Weinerville and wolfed down four or five dogs." (Parker bikes twenty miles a day when he's not traveling. "I exercise so that I can eat. Period." He also drinks three liters of water a day. That's the health regimen that supports his incredible work regimen.) The day before I saw him, he'd tasted 150 wines for his newsletter. How he is able to do this—and to evaluate and remember each of them—has been the subject of much speculation. Is he one of those rare "super-tasters," born with more taste buds on his tongue? Parker himself is skeptical, although he notes that his father had an exceptionally keen sense of smell. "I may have inherited a particularly acute olfactory instrument," he suggests.

Parker may be a hedonist, but he's also a missionary. He sees himself as a reformer, a consumer advocate, the Martin Luther of the wine world. The name of his newsletter is revealing: no mere *Spectator* he. "There's an inherent conflict between oenologists and consumers," he says. Since the beginning of his career, Parker has railed against the cozy relationship between wine writers and the trade, particularly in England, where many wine writers were—and continue to be—involved in the sale and distribution of wine. One well-known English critic was reputed to leave the trunk of his car open when he visited wineries—as a helpful hint. Except for unsolicited bottle samples, Parker accepts no freebies of any kind, whether travel, lodging, or wine. And his newsletter accepts no advertising. Partly as a result, *The Wine Advocate*, despite a worldwide paid subscription of just forty thousand, is the most influential wine publication in the world.

Parker's critics complain about his influence and his taste, the standard rap being that he likes big, floozy, in-your-face wines saturated with new oak, and that his power has resulted in an "international style" that ignores the nuances of grape varietal and geography. There's no question, Parker likes big wines. On the other hand, his favorite wines for personal consumption are southern Rhônes, particularly Châteauneuf-du-Pape. As he is quick to point out, the wines of Château Rayas, Château de Beaucastel, and Henri Bonneau are quirky artisanal wines made with little new oak. And when he decided to invest in an Oregon winery, Beaux Frères, with his brother-in-law, Mike Etzel, he chose that daintiest of grapes—Pinot Noir.

Old World critics sometimes accuse Parker of favoring California-style super-ripe wines like the '82 Bordeaux vintage, which helped make his reputation. But he has long been a critic of the overly technological U.C. Davis approach that has predominated in the New World until recently. His campaign against filtration, which he believes strips a wine of character for the sake of stability, has been so successful that the word *unfiltered* is now displayed on many premium wine labels.

Asked to describe the much discussed "Parker Effect" on the wine world, he says without a moment's hesitation: "Lower yields, ripe fruit, an artisanal approach. Less is better. Let the *terroir* express itself. This is my legacy." If this sounds a little technical, let me put it this way: The next time you open a bottle of wine, raise the first glass to Robert Parker, because, no matter what it is, it will probably taste better than it would have if the big man had stuck with corporate law.

MONDAVI ON MONDAVI*

Not so long ago the phrase *California wine* belonged in the same book of oxymorons as, say, *living poet* and *Dutch cuisine*. You knew, on some level, that such things existed, but you didn't necessarily want any of them at your dinner table. Today, thirty-two years after Robert Mondavi founded his eponymous winery in the Napa Valley, wine has become California's second most glamorous export and Napa has become one of the world's celebrated wine regions. Just ask Mondavi's neighbor, winemaker Francis Ford Coppola.

Wine buffs and collectors from around the world put their names on waiting lists in the hope of acquir-

*A review of *Harvest of Joy*, a memoir by Robert Mondavi.

ing a few bottles of the latest boutique Cabernet from Colgin or Screaming Eagle. A personalized Napa Valley winery has become a popular trophy for American plutocrats, and the formerly rustic town of St. Helena brims with the kind of polo-shirted tourists who also seek out Aspen and Santa Fe. And all of those tourists, like many of their fellow Americans, know how to pronounce *Cabernet Sauvignon*. In his booster-ish memoir, *Harvest of Joy*, Mondavi doesn't take any more credit than he deserves for these developments.

Like his dowdier peers Ernest and Julio Gallo, Mondavi was the son of Italian immigrants. His father emigrated to Minnesota and, after a stint in the iron mines, opened a grocery store in a mining town called Virginia, where Robert and his younger brother Peter were born. His description of their childhood might best be characterized as polenta pone—"Family, hard work, high spirits, healthy, hearty meals—my child-hood was a daily infusion of all four." With the enactment of the Volstead Act in 1919, Mondavi se-nior became involved in the grape business; under the terms of Prohibition, families were permitted to make two hundred gallons of wine for home consumption, and the Italian residents of Virginia, Minnesota, elected to do just that, appointing Cesare Mondavi as their representative to travel to California and buy grapes to be shipped north. When Robert was ten, Cesare moved the family to Lodi, California, "the grape capital of the United States," where he became a wholesaler of grapes and eventually, after repeal, the co-owner of a Napa Valley winery called Sunny St. Helena. Made from purchased grapes, the Sunny St. Helena product was pressed, fermented, and shipped out in railroad tank cars.

When Robert joined the family business in 1936, after graduating from Stanford, viticulture in the Napa Valley was a marginal enterprise. Fifty years before, Napa seemed well on its way to oenological stardom. A tiny root louse, *Phylloxera vastatris*, had almost completely destroyed the vineyards of France, creating an opportunity for California viticulture. In the late 1870s state-of-the-art wineries were established by German immigrant Jacob Beringer and a Helsinki fur trader named Gustave Niebaum. Niebaum's Inglenook and Beringer Brothers were among the pioneers of a frenzied Napa grape rush; by 1887 more than sixteen thousand acres of Napa were under the vine, at which point the dread phylloxera struck the valley. Just when the root louse was being brought under control, along came the tambourines of the temperance movement. The dark ages of Prohibition and the depression crippled the fledgling industry. Some of the wineries that had survived by selling grapes and altar wine damaged the image of California wines by shipping spoiled juice they had been holding during the dry years. In contrast to the U.C. Davis–trained oeno-geeks who would conquer the valley in the 1970s and 1980s, most winemakers barely understood the chemistry of fermentation, according to wine historian James T. Lapsley, "and they lacked the technology to control it even if they did." Most wineries were undercapitalized; there was no national network for wine sales and distribution. And there were few consumers. The immigrants who considered wine a staple of daily life often made their own. Most of the wine coming out of California, whether in bottles or tank cars, was a sweet beverage of the type that is now most commonly associated with brown paper sacks. Produced from high-yielding, inferior grape varietals, it was unlikely ever to appeal to those few Americans who appreciated the complex, dry wines of Burgundy and Bordeaux, although, to the irritation of the French wine industry, they often bore French names like Chablis and Burgundy. A few visionaries, like Inglenook's Carl Bundschu and Beaulieu's André Tchelistcheff, recognized the great potential of the Napa Valley and even succeeded, on occasion, in proving it.

A former Russian aristocrat who fought with Kerenskey, Tchelistcheff was a trained agronomist who fled to France, where he studied microbiology at the Pasteur Institute while holding down a series of jobs in the French wine industry. In 1937 he was hired as a winemaker by Georges de Latour, a native of Bordeaux who had become wealthy selling French rootstock to California grape growers and purchased a Napa estate at the turn of the century. Tchelistcheff brought French winemaking expertise and a sense of high purpose to the Napa Valley. He was among the first to import the French concept of *terroir* to the valley; hundreds of years of grape growing had allowed the

French to parse the viticultural landscape into hundreds of regions and subregions based on nuances of soil type and microclimate. Tchelistcheff attempted to do something similar in Napa, identifying at least three climatic regions in the valley and replanting the Beaulieu vineyards with the grapes he deemed most suitable. From the end of the 1930s until the 1970s, his George de Latour Private Reserve Cabernet Sauvignon was a benchmark. Among those inspired by Tchelistcheff was Robert Mondavi. Mondavi hired Tchelistcheff as a consultant when his family purchased the venerable Charles Krug winery in 1943 and turned to him again when he went off on his own. Despite some hands-on winemaking experience, Mondavi has never really been the man in the cellar, but he has been very smart, and fortunate, in hiring winemaking talent. The valley is rife with Mondavi alumni, including such superstars as Warren Winiarski, Mike Grgich, Zelma Long, and Helen Turley. At Krug it was his younger brother Peter who assumed the winemaking responsibilities. Robert was Mr. Outside, the public face of the Krug Winery, a tireless promoter of his own product and the Napa Valley in general. In 1952 Krug was among the first wineries to establish a tasting room for visitors. He traveled the country glad-handing restaurant owners and distributors.

The power struggle between the two Mondavi brothers and the departure of Robert from the Charles Krug Winery has become, in the lore of the valley, the local Cain and Abel legend. As Robert tells the story in

Harvest of Joy, it all began when he first visited the great wine regions of Europe in 1962 and experienced an oenological epiphany. After touring the Old World châteaux and tasting the great wines of Bordeaux and Burgundy on their home *terroir,* he recalls, "a great business and creative venture took shape before my eyes: I wanted to take American technology, management techniques, and marketing savvy and fuse them together with Old World tradition and elegance in the art of making fine wine." The older brother arrived back in Napa all fired up: "I wanted my family and our company to commit ourselves to a true quest for excellence in our vineyards, in our wine making, and in our marketing and sales." By his own account, Robert was unable to interest the rest of the family in his vision. (His father had died in 1959.) In his history of Napa Valley winemaking, *Bottled Poetry,* James T. Lapsley basically confirms Robert's version: "One of the major differences between Robert and Peter Mondavi had been whether to continue to reinvest profits into expanding Charles Krug, as opposed to distributing to family members."

In the end, according to Robert, it was a mink coat that started the war. As the public face of the Krug Winery, Robert received an invitation from President John F. Kennedy to attend a state dinner at the White House. "Flattered though we were, Marge and I were very nervous. . . . We were just small-town people running a small family business . . . how in the world would we fare at the Kennedy White House, with the charismatic president and his famous wife, surrounded by all the glamour of Camelot? Marge also had a more specific worry: what in the dickens should she wear to a White House dinner? What dress? What shoes? What bag? What jewelry? What coat?" Mondavi's admirers as well as his detractors will probably be astonished at this self-portrait of the King of Napa Valley as an awkward charisma-phobe. About the shoes and dress we learn nothing, but the couple eventually settled on a mink coat from I. Magnin in San Francisco. "When he heard about that mink, my brother Peter went into a snit." The snit became a sulk that simmered until it became a fistfight two years later. At one of those big family gatherings that are so conducive to the airing of grievances, Peter accused Robert of spending too much money on travel and promotion. Then he accused his older brother of taking money from the winery. How else, he demanded, could Robert have afforded to buy the mink coat?

" 'Say that again and I'll hit you,' " Robert warned his younger brother. "He said it again. Then I gave him a third chance.

" 'Take it back.'

" 'No.'

"So I smacked him, hard. Twice."

Robert and Peter were eventually separated by bystanders; the rift was never healed. Many years later the older brother would triumph in the acrimonious lawsuit that followed. In the meantime, since the other family members sided with Peter, Robert was, at the age of fifty-two, out of the family business. He decided to go back and start from scratch in pursuing his quixotic vision of producing world-class Napa Valley wines. It was a daunting, practically ludicrous mission; quite aside from the question of capital, in 1965 there was still no significant American market for the kind of fine wine Mondavi hoped to produce. Julia Child was still trying to wean Americans away from tuna casseroles and chipped beef. On the other hand, as everyone had long observed, the weather in Napa was practically perfect for ripening grapes, whereas the growers in Bordeaux and Burgundy enjoyed, at best, three great vintage years a decade.

After purchasing a piece of a well-situated old vineyard called To Kalon, Mondavi turned his attention to designing a winery that would make a statement. His architect, Cliff May, wanted to place the Mission-style winery with its faux campanile far back against the hills, but Mondavi opted for a spot within sight of Highway 29, where its yawning archway would presumably attract visitors and serve as a kind of billboard for the enterprise. Its silhouette, which graces the labels of Robert Mondavi estate wines, has since become iconic, at least as recognizable to wine lovers as that of the Bell Tower at Château Latour. Inside the winery Mondavi presided over a series of technological innovations. He was among the first to grasp the importance of steel tanks and cold fermentation in the making of crisp, untainted white wines. He also pioneered, in this country, the use of new French oak casks for imparting more complex flavor and structure to Cabernet Sauvignon.

The latter practice, which is now considered de rigueur for serious Cabernets, he had observed at the great châteaux of Bordeaux. Mondavi embraced technology wherever he could, happily calling his "the test-tube winery." In the past the California wine industry had been plagued by spoilage; in the attempt to make a clean, stable product, Mondavi and those who followed him went too far down the road of sanitation—filtering and sterilizing the living beverage almost to death. "Only later did we discover that this rigorous cleaning—what we call the suppression of fault—robbed wine of vital essences, flavor and character." Not surprisingly, America's first great wine region tended, in the eyes of its critics, to rely too heavily on science in the form of fertilizers, filters, and additives. Mondavi was quicker to dial back some of this technology than many who adhered to the high-tech gospel of the Oenology Department of the University of California at Davis, which became a combination think tank and training ground for the industry.

Ironically, Mondavi played no direct role in the great event that certified the arrival of the Napa Valley as a major wine region, the famed "Judgment of Paris." In 1976 a British wine connoisseur named Steven Spurrier organized a blind-tasting in Paris that pitted some of the most venerable French wines from Burgundy and Bordeaux against some of the Napa Valley upstarts. Spurrier made a trip to Napa to hand-pick the American entrants. California Chardonnays were competing against white Burgundies—which are also made from Chardonnay and are generally regarded as the highest expression of that grape; California Cabernets were matched against some of the greatest Cabernet-based wines of Bordeaux, including Château Mouton-Rothschild and Haut-Brion. All nine judges were French, and their oenological credentials were impeccable, which made the results all the more surprising—and embarrassing for the Frogs. The top-scoring white wine was Mike Grgich's '73 Château Montelena Chardonnay. Two of the other top four white wines chosen were American. The winner in the red category was Warren Winiarski's 1973 Stag's Leap Wine Cellar Cabernet. Naturally, the French were indignant. The French press at first ignored the results and later tried to explain them away. One or two of these dozens of explanations were even remotely plausible. French *grand vin* tends to be made for the long haul and to show more awkwardly in youth than the ripe, buxom, flirty wines of California. On the other hand, the patriotic tasters would presumably have been on the lookout for hints of California glitz. At any rate, the Spurrier tasting made an enormous impression on both sides of the Atlantic. Mondavi professes himself "tickled to death by the outcome." Whatever frustration he felt at sitting out the big event must have been ameliorated by the fact that the two winners, Grgich and Winiarski, were alumni of his cellars. And his vision for the industry had been resoundingly endorsed.

Mondavi continued to expand and proselytize, seeming less like a voice in the wilderness. His '74 Cabernet Sauvignon Reserve, released around the time of the great tasting, has become something of a legend. And in 1978 the French came calling. Baron Philippe de Rothschild, proprietor of Mouton-Rothschild, invited Mondavi to participate in a joint venture in the Napa Valley. If Mondavi still needed vindication, this, presumably, was it. Indeed, he can scarcely conceal his pride. "My parents came to America without a penny in their pockets. Now, thanks to hard work and the ability to turn humble grapes into fine wine, the names Rothschild and Mondavi were going to stand side by side." The venture nearly capsized; huge cost overruns plagued the limestone-clad postmodern winery, and consumers were initially skeptical about the wine when it was released at fifty dollars a bottle. And then, just a year after the first vineyards were planted, phylloxera struck again. The dread root louse swept through the valley over the next decade, wiping out millions of dollars' worth of vines. The new epidemic was a mixed curse: It cost millions to replant the vineyards, but the new plantings tended to be genetically superior and to reflect advances in the understanding of climate, soil, and grape types.

The cost of replanting was one of the reasons Mondavi decided, in one of his typically bold moves, to take the winery public in 1993. Shortly afterward, he appointed his son Michael president, possibly ending a long power struggle between Michael and his younger brother Tim which threatened to become a replay of the earlier family feud at Charles Krug. In *Harvest of Joy* Mondavi only hints at these family dramas behind the corporate success story.

He confesses that his fierce and single-minded ambition damaged his family without really showing us how. The portrait of his saintly, silent wife Marge is typical; after buying the mink, she more or less disappears from the narrative. The reader is occasionally puzzled by flattering references to a Mondavi employee named Margrit Biever until, near the end of the book, Mondavi mentions that she became his second wife. And we learn little about his sons, who will lead this hugely successful company into the new century. One senses, if not a *King Lear,* certainly a *Rich Man, Poor Man* of a story here, waiting for its bard. If *Harvest of Joy* were a wine, we would have to say that it was a little disjointed, lacked complexity, and had too much residual sugar. But then it's entirely fitting that Mondavi's most eloquent message still comes in a bottle.

THE BARON OF
BARBARESCO

Angelo Gaja is a man in a hurry. He talks fast. He walks fast. And he drives like Jackie Stewart on crystal meth. Trying to follow the taillights of his BMW 750 through the hairpin turns of a back road in Piedmont outside Barbaresco is a hair-raising experience. I console myself with the fact that if I plummet over the edge, I will die in the middle of one or another of the world's finest—and steepest—vineyards, preferably one of Gaja's. When I finally reach Da Cesare, the restaurant that is our destination, Gaja is donning the jacket of an impeccably cut double-breasted suit, looking crisp as he carefully fastens the buttons and then checks his watch. "Oh, dear, are you warm?" he asks, frowning with genuine concern as I stagger out of my rented

Opel on wobbly legs, drenched in sweat. Gaja takes the well-being of visitors to Piedmont personally: If he could rebuke the local weather at this moment, I'm sure he would.

At fifty-nine, Gaja shows no sign of slowing down. Since he took over his father's estate in the late 1960s, he's almost single-handedly turned Barbaresco—a formerly rustic, indifferently made, locally consumed *vino*—into one of the world's great names in wine, to the point where it threatens to overshadow Barolo, its more venerated sibling. He has done this partly by a fanatic devotion to quality in his vineyards and cellars—cutting yields, selecting and aging the oak for his own barrels, and selecting the bark for his corks—and partly by driving and flying around the world to promote the wines.

Over the past thirty years Gaja has given the wines of Barbaresco, and Italian wines in general, a new credibility, much as his friend and mentor Robert Mondavi did for the wines of the Napa Valley and the rest of California. "It's fantastic what Mondavi did for California," he says, *fantastic* being one of his favorite English words. "He saw the potential before anyone else. Also here he saw the potential, when he comes to visit in 1973. He says that everyone in the Langhe is sleeping. And he's right. We were all sleeping. Fantastic!" (The fact that he's told this tale at least a hundred times before doesn't seem to diminish his enthusiasm.) I find it hard to believe that Gaja has ever spent much time sleeping. Nor does he watch television; not too long ago, after deciding that his three children were watching too much of it, he took the television out to the courtyard of his winery and ceremonially disassembled it with the help of a sledgehammer.

Despite his obvious enthusiasm for food and wine—he keeps urging me to try different dishes—there is something ascetic and highly disciplined about Gaja, who is so fastidious that he stains the center sections of his barrels red in order to avoid the uneven staining that occurs around the bungholes when wine samples are removed. Over the course of three meals, I observe that he eats and drinks sparingly. "I spend a great deal of time eating and drinking for business," he says, explaining his restraint. But one gets the feeling that Gaja doesn't want to cloud his focus. His cheerful intensity is almost overwhelming as he describes his new vineyards in Bolgheri (home of the Super Tuscan Sassicaia and Ornellaia), his new winery in Montalcino (of Brunello fame), and the luxury inn he is creating from a medieval castle in his tiny hometown of Barbaresco (pop. 630), across the street from his winery.

If there is a dichotomy in the soul of Angelo Gaja, it is that of the local farmer who is also an international figure. Although his family is originally from Spain, they have lived in the hills of Piedmont for two hundred years. His first love as a winemaker is the Nebbiolo grape, which is cranky and temperamental enough to make Pinot Noir seem like Doris Day, and which seems to thrive, if it can ever be said to thrive, only in the steep hills of Piedmont. The wine from Barbaresco and nearby Barolo is traditionally extremely slow to mature and difficult for a foreign palate to understand, characterized at its best by wonderful aromas that are often said to evoke tar and roses. They are, like most Italian wines, best appreciated with food, a fact that Gaja says makes it difficult to show them in blind-tastings against fruitier foreign varietals, although his own Nebbiolo-based wines inevitably garner stellar scores from the critics.

Gaja made a name for himself by applying French practices—particularly the use of new-oak barrels—to the vinification of Nebbiolo, which initially raised deep suspicion in the area. But his greatest crime against local sensibilities was to reintroduce "foreign" grapes like Chardonnay and Cabernet Sauvignon to the area. Now, with his purchase of new estates, first in Barolo and then in Tuscany, he is branching out even farther from his roots.

If anyone can pull off this kind of expansion without diluting quality, it's Gaja. I visited his new estate, Pieve Santa Restituta, in Montalcino, which, until Gaja stole the spotlight for Piedmont, was the most internationally renowned wine region in Italy. His '95 and '96 vintages are as good as anything being made there, although traditionalists will complain, no doubt, as they did in Barbaresco, about his use of new oak. Touring the vineyard, though, it was easy to see one source of the quality: As much fruit lay on the ground—pruned away—as on the vines themselves. Dropping fruit lowers yields and concentrates the flavors of the remaining clusters, but this kind of dedication to quality doesn't come cheap.

The chief complaint against Gaja's wines is their expense; the single-vineyard Barbarescos are released at more than a hundred dollars a bottle, about as much as Grand Cru Burgundies and first-growth Bordeaux. Demand for the exceptional '95, '96, and '97 vintages can only boost prices further. "The pursuit of perfection comes at a price," he explains wearily. Gaja's been hearing complaints about prices ever since his father first decided to charge twice as much as the other growers did. When Angelo first presented his wines in the United States, one wine critic at a gathering in Boston asked about prices. "When he heard them," Gaja recalls, "he says, this is ridiculous to charge for an Italian wine. He walks out in disgust." Gaja pauses. "That was before he tasted the wine. Then we became friends." Were there not so many reasons to like Gaja, I might suspect this critic of having befriended him in order to secure a line of supply for the wines. For, as you will discover, finding them is only slightly less difficult than keeping up with Gaja on a winding mountain road. But I'd take that drive again any day, if there was a bottle of his Barbaresco waiting at my destination.

THE WIZARD OF BOLINAS

The turnoff to Bolinas from the coast highway is unmarked. Not that the California Department of Transportation hasn't tried to mark it, but whenever it puts up a sign, it's gone within hours. The people of Bolinas don't want to be found, and you can hardly blame them when you see this seaside town with its Victorian cottages and its Age of Aquarius ambience. At Smiley's bar the dress code is 1968. Bolinas was once known as a doper's town, but I've come in search of fine wine.

The first sight of Sean Thackrey's backyard winery is hardly reassuring. The place looks like a cross between a small Zen monastery and a junkyard. Obscure machinery rusts in the shade of the fragrant, towering eucalyptus trees. Barrels and barrel staves litter the property. An egret flies low through a stand of Monterey pines. The only sound is a faint gurgle from the redwood fermentation tanks. This definitely ain't the Robert Mondavi tasting room, Toto.

The proprietor eventually appears. Sean Thackrey has a seriously weathered, friendly face and the shambling, intense manner of a mad scientist—or of a Celtic wizard stirring his bubbling cauldrons. Tasting with him from the barrels—some of which are sheltered from the elements in a kind of Quonset hut and some of which are simply stacked in the yard—one half expects him to cackle, "Needs a little more eye of newt." Earthy as they are, Thackrey's wines are always named for constellations. "I've been standing out in vineyards at night under a completely starry sky," he explains, "and that relation between stars and clusters of ripe grapes has meant a lot to me. If you will, it's a symbol of the antiquity and mystery of my craft, which I could have practiced essentially unchanged in the Sumeria of the Gilgamesh epic."

While he dislikes the term, Thackrey is sometimes identified as one of California's Rhône Rangers, so called for their use of varietals associated with France's Rhône Valley. "Syrah," suggests wine critic Jancis Robinson, "may be even better suited to the climate of northern California than Cabernet Sauvignon." It's a powerful, film-noir kind of grape, yielding—in the hands of makers like Bonny Doon, Edmunds St. John, Neyers, and Dehlinger—a burly, smoky, and spicy wine that cries out for grilled lamb, game birds, and venison. Thackrey's old-vine Syrah '89 Orion, which I drank recently with a marinated flank steak, was so stunningly rich and complex, it drove me to his doorstep.

The Wine Enthusiast named Thackrey's '92 Sirius the best red wine in the world for 1996. Unfortunately, '92 was the last vintage. Thackrey doesn't own a vineyard and is forced to rely on purchased grapes; his wines are so good that the deep-pocket wineries seem to follow him around and buy the vineyards out from under him. "The original vineyard for Orion," he tells me, "was bought by W. Clark Swanson Jr. of Swanson Vineyards because he liked the wine so much." In the case of Sirius, Nestlé-owned mega-winery Beringer was the culprit. "In the middle of this very large vineyard," Thackrey recalls, "was a patch of Petite Syrah, which was then a very unfashionable grape." The owner got an offer from Beringer he apparently couldn't refuse. The Petite Syrah (or *Petite Sirah,* as it is usually spelled) patch, which probably dated back to the turn of the century, was promptly ripped up, and that was the end of Sirius. "I used to call it Sirius Old Vines," Thackrey says. "For the final vintage, I changed it to Sirius Doomed Vines."

Two and a half hours from his main vineyard in St. Helena, Bolinas may not be the most practical location for Thackrey's winery, but figuratively it's the perfect place for this hippie David tilting against the yuppie Goliaths of Napa. A former art dealer, Thackrey moved to Bolinas in 1963. His first vintage was made from Cabernet Sauvignon grapes purchased from a shop called Wine and the People in Berkeley, which sold grapes and equipment to home winemakers. "It was like someone going to the piano for the first time," he says, "and realizing they had a feel for it." When asked if he has any formal training, Thackrey likes to say, "Yes, in art history." In Thackrey's cosmology, you gather, U.C. Davis occupies a position contiguous to Beringer.

The self-taught virtuoso is a serious scholar of the history of winemaking. He's working his way through a 1545 French edition of the Twenty Books of Agriculture of the Emperor Constantine of Byzantium. "It's the only compendium of winemaking between the end of the Roman Empire and the early medieval period. Supposedly compiled in the seventh century. Fascinating—the most bizarre bunch of nonsense imaginable." Another recent find is *Maison Rustique, or the Country Farme,* a 1616 translation of a French encyclopedia of agriculture. He's already read the book in French but is enjoying the Elizabethan English. "My long-term object is to write an informal history of winemaking." In the meantime, he occasionally experiments with the lore of his ancient predecessors.

Like so many before it, Thackrey's just-released '95 Orion is an amazing wine, spicy and smoky, paradoxically powerful and elegant—Robert Mitchum and Maurice Chevalier. Worth killing—or dancing—for. Thackrey makes about five hundred cases of Orion and up to fifteen hundred cases of a complex, Syrah-based, nonvintage blend called Pleiades. It takes a bit of wizardry on the consumer's part to conjure up bottles of these wines. You can try Don's Liquors in Bolinas. If you manage to find the town, just don't tell them I sent you.

ATTITUDE? NON!
(ON SOMMELIER JEAN LUC LE DU)

The only two things that have ever spoiled a bottle of '85 Lynch-Bages for me are: 1. kissing a check scented with a liberal dose of Jean Patou, and 2. a snotty sommelier at Lucas Carton in Paris. The phrase *snotty sommelier* may seem like a redundancy; certainly in Paris it's a given. And it's not just us guys with the bad accents who get abused. "When I go to France," says Jean-Luc Le Du, "a lot of times I don't even talk to the sommeliers, they're so snobbish." Not only is Jean-Luc French, he's also the sommelier at Daniel Boulud's Manhattan Restaurant Daniel, one of the greatest temples of haute cuisine on the planet.

Until recently, the relative lack of sommeliers in American restaurants could be interpreted as a blessing.

If you manage to snag a reservation at a place like Daniel and are prepared to stress your credit card accordingly, chances are you don't want some twit wearing an ashtray around his neck to make you feel like an idiot. On the other hand, faced with a wine list the size of a John Irving novel, you may be grateful for editorial guidance. Of course, any media mogul can order the '61 Château Pétrus. Safe bet. Daniel sometimes sells several of them in a week, at six thousand dollars a pop. You don't need Jean-Luc to tell you it's good. (Though he prefers the '61 Latour-à-Pomerol.) Where a good sommelier comes in handy is in selecting a slightly less illustrious wine and matching it to your food.

I first became as enthusiastic about Jean-Luc as he is about wine when he made me feel like a genius for ordering a fifty-dollar Languedoc ('89 Prieuré de Saint-Jean de Bébian)—even though it was his idea to begin with. "Great choice—this is fantastic wine," he said, beaming at me. *Fantastic* is probably Jean-Luc's favorite wine descriptor. Reserve and hauteur are not part of his repertoire. He bounces when he gets excited. It's hard for him to suppress his enthusiasm for the wines on Daniel's list. At thirty-two, he hardly appears old enough to drink legally in New York. He does not wear a *tastevin* (the sterling-silver tasting thing traditionally worn from a chain around the neck), and initially you may mistake him for a scholarly busboy or for a live-action version of young Sherman from the Rocky and Bullwinkle cartoons. But just ask him a question, and you will discover that where wine is concerned, he is a lover and a scholar.

"Didier Dagueneau, he is one of my favorite makers," he effervesces one night, "very eccentric, fantastic wines. He races dogsleds—how do you call them?—huskies. This is a beautiful wine, perfect for your scallops." Somehow, I don't know why, that dogsled detail seems useful. The wine in question is nothing if not racy.

Though many of the wines he loves are French, Jean-Luc did not discover them until he came to the States. He was born in Brittany, "the land of no vines." His parents didn't drink wine and neither, growing up, did he. After a stint in biz school, he came to New York at nineteen because he loved rock and roll. Not long after arriving in the States, he visited an aunt who lived in Queens for Thanksgiving dinner. A relative brought a bottle of '64 Cheval Blanc to the festivities. For young Jean-Luc, it was love at first sip. "I can still taste that wine in my mouth," he says of the revelation. "I couldn't believe something could taste that good." The next day he bought several wine books, including *Alexis Lichine's Guide to the Wines and Vineyards of France.* His guitar started to gather dust.

In the course of earning a living and pursuing his new passion Jean-Luc worked at various restaurants, including the Carlyle and the late great Bouley, where he eventually became captain. Though he has never taken a wine course, he was named best sommelier in the Northeast in last year's prestigious SOPEXA competition.

"There never used to be sommeliers in New York," he says. "And you could tell by looking at the wine lists. All the Burgundies came from the big *négotiant* houses. The chefs and maître d's didn't have the time to seek out the smaller wines." Jean-Luc spends dozens of hours a week tasting, tracking down rarities, perusing catalogues, attending auctions, and wooing small distributors over the phone. Sometimes, for a special customer, a last-minute phone call is placed to secure a rare bottle from "a guy who can get anything—at a price."

Officially, Jean-Luc's day begins before lunch, when he consults with chef Daniel—a wine expert himself—about the menu. Sometime after midnight he returns home to Brooklyn, where he reads about wine until three or four in the morning. Fortunately, he says, his American-born wife, Evelyn, shares his enthusiasm. (One hopes so, for her sake.) Their holidays are spent in the Loire and other wine regions, seeking out new vinous treasures. Though the list at Daniel features many of the great wines of Bordeaux and Burgundy, he gets a special buzz from hidden treasures like Clos Erasmus from Spain, in part because "that is what I can afford to drink myself."

Among the ideal qualifications for a sommelier are a photographic memory and the ability to read minds. A friend of mine from Los Angeles recently returned to Daniel after six months. He had forgotten the name of a wine he'd loved on his last visit. Jean-Luc not only remembered the guy, he remembered all four wines that he'd ordered that night. Uncannily, he seems to sense what my price range might be on any given night. Those who don't trust his psychic abilities can point to a wine in the desired price range: A good sommelier will take the hint. A good sommelier will also, he says, keep his mouth shut if his advice is not requested. This may be the hardest part of the job for the ebullient Jean-Luc, who likes nothing better than to share his passion.

Some sommeliers will pretaste a wine for a customer—hence the *tastevin*. Jean-Luc considers this a somewhat pretentious ritual. Along with his guitar, his *tastevin* stays back home in Brooklyn. He uses it as an ashtray.

THE HOST

Driving up the D2 through Bordeaux, I feel much the way others might as they cruise Mulholland Drive with a "Map of the Stars' Homes" pinned to the steering wheel. I'm completely starstruck when I see the signs of the great winemaking châteaux: Lynch-Bages, Léoville Las Cases, Latour. Not the least advantage that Bordeaux enjoys over Beverly Hills is the architecture—the grand châteaux that rise from the left bank of the Gironde River. One of the most impressive of these is Château Ducru Beaucaillou, in Saint-Julien, which sits far back from the road amid a grove of ancient trees, a neoclassical palace punctuated at either end by a square tower.

From the road it would be difficult to imagine some of the sleek, minimalist interiors of Ducru's southern tower, the residence of Bruno Borie, second son of the proprietor. Bruno's grandfather bought the old château in 1941 and spent some twenty years restoring it. More recently, forty-two-year-old Bruno has carried the restoration of his own part of the house into the twenty-first century, designing along the way a bloodred octagonal dining room and a master bathroom the size of a Tribeca loft, which houses part of his contemporary art collection. But it's the ground-floor, nineteenth-century harvest kitchen that is the heart of Borie's bachelor pad. Borie owns Lillet, makers of the famous aperitif, and also runs much of the family wine business, although if you ask him what his title is, he replies, with characteristic wry self-deprecation, "Son." I'm having business cards made for him inscribed with the title HOST, for he seems nowhere as happy as he is in the kitchen, wearing an apron and swinging a whisk, single-handedly preparing a meal for ten or twelve friends and then presiding over the table. On less populous occasions he likes to fire up a bundle of gnarled old grapevines from the vineyard outside and grill T-bone steaks. A guest will often find a bottle of Ducru from his birth year standing beside his glass.

Not the least of the pleasures of the harvest, for Borie, is the preparation of the traditional harvest meal—a pot-au-feu. Traditionally the dish was prepared midharvest for the pickers and the cellar workers. "You sacrifice a cow," says Borie. "It's an important ritual of the harvest." In his charcoal gray bespoke suit, pouring a glass of Château d'Yquem into my glass the night before the big pot-au-feu lunch, he doesn't look like a man who has any truck with cattle butchery. But the next morning, wearing his chef's whites, he seems intimate with cow parts that I've never ever seen before. To mark the conclusion of the 1997 harvest Borie has invited for lunch his friends from the Jeune Toquaise, a group of local women who share an interest in food and wine.

"It's about memory," says Borie, stirring the broth in the bath-sized pot.

"For me it is memories of past harvests. Every pot-au-feu you have afterward, if I succeed, you will remember this one." I hope he's right. I have never quite gotten over my own set of memories concerning boiled beef and vegetables; the product of an Irish Catholic family, I was subjected to corned beef and cabbage several times a month growing up. Despite a few subsequent lunches at Le Cirque, pot-au-feu has always seemed to me about as exciting as macaroni and cheese. Until today, that is. Although he had hosted a rather grand dinner party for ten in his raspberry-colored octagonal dining room the night before, Bruno starts preparing lunch at seven in the morning. By ten, when I stagger in, the kitchen is redolent with an intoxicating *eau de boeuf*. Also carrots, potatoes, and celery. I'm still under the sensory influence of last night's mocha-scented 1953 Ducru Beaucaillou. I've liked Ducru for years—the '78 was one of the first serious wines I ever had. The vineyard takes its name in part from its terrain's numerous pebbles—*beaucaillou* meaning "beautiful pebbles"—which tend to hold the heat of the sun and radiate it to the vines well into the night. Ranked as a second growth in the famous 1855 classification, Ducru is currently considered one of the "super seconds" that are almost on a par with the first growths. Ducru has always been a wine of finesse rather than sheer brute power, a kind of Burgundian Bordeaux. Since the creation of a state-of-the-art winery in 1990, the quality has only improved; '95 and '96 are among the greatest wines made here—or anywhere in Bordeaux, for that matter.

An hour before the lunching ladies arrive Bruno is chopping shallots for the dipping sauce, which also includes tomatoes, garlic, estragon, ciboulet, lemons, and capers. He holds out a wooden spoon for me. "Try our local ketchup," he says.

"It's great," I respond. "What's it called?"

He raises one eyebrow, rather like a Gallic version of P. G. Wodehouse's Jeeves. "Tomato sauce," he answers, as he stirs the pot.

Shortly before the arrival of the lunch club, I get to taste the broth, which I am surprised to learn is served separately, before the meat and vegetables. "You always separate the broth," Bruno assures me. As a wine buff I find that this makes sense, since wine and soup are such a tricky combo. Drinking the broth first, with a glass of Evian, allows a clearer field for the '94 Haut-Batailley— another Borie property—that follows. All thoughts of

New England corned beef and cabbage dinners are banished at first sip. This is probably the finest unfermented liquid I have ever put in my mouth, right up there with last night's '53 Ducru Beaucaillou. The meat and vegetables, when I get to them, are also excellent, particularly in the company of the sauce.

My high opinion of the pot-au-feu is shared by the members of the Jeune Toquaise, which might just as accurately be styled the "Blond Toquaise." The group is made up of ten Chaneled and Valentinoed women who like to cook and eat. They also like to talk politics and business. Their ranks include doctors, businesswomen, a wine critic, and the wife of Bruno's older brother, Jean Eugene, the genial and wizardly winemaker for Ducru Beaucaillou. This is, from the chef's point of view, a tough crowd, but they reward Bruno with an ovation. When the meal is finished and the conversation turns to matchmaking, Bruno slips outdoors for a contemplative smoke at the edge of the vineyard. The vines stretch from the house to the river in orderly rows, like a green battalion marching on the château. I take the opportunity to ask him about the rosebushes that mark the end of each row of vines like pink flags—a common sight in Bordeaux vineyards.

"There are three theories about that," he tells me. "One is that the roses were like the canaries in the coal mines—early-warning systems for disease. Another theory is that they were planted so that the horses would know when to turn, at the end of each row."

"And the third theory?"

He smiles and takes a long drag. "Perhaps they're just there because they're beautiful," he says. "We have forgotten about gratuitous acts of beauty."

Apparently, some of us haven't forgotten.

ON DOING IT RIGHT

APROPOS THE APERITIF

"... they had drunk cocktails before meals like Americans, wines and brandies like Frenchmen, beer like Germans, whiskey-and-soda like the English."
—F. Scott Fitzgerald, "The Bridal Party"

I have nothing against cocktails. Far from it. A martini is my idea of a great way to kick-start the night. On the other hand, from the point of view of your liver as well as your taste buds, a high-octane cocktail or two can be too much of a good thing if you're planning to kill some serious wine with dinner. The French—and the Italians—unlike Fitzgerald's Jazz Age expatriates, have always been cognizant of this fact. Hence the aperitif, a Gallic concept that strikes me as far more compelling than, say, the bidet.

The aperitif is foreplay. The point is to tease your taste buds instead of mauling them, to set up a light buzz of anticipation for incipient pleasures, to stimulate the tongue rather than thickening it. The ideal aperitif contains hints of bitterness along with sweetness and underlying acidity—thus exercising three of the four zones of taste perceptions (saltiness is the fourth), prepping your tongue for the big game to come. When in Rome—or Milan—I like to follow local custom and start things off with a Campari and soda, or a Martini Bianco on the rocks. The latter, Martini and Rossi's semisweet vermouth, is very refreshing, though not always available at your local saloon. Campari has a wonderful syrupy texture—hence the soda— and a bitter backbite that for me brings back fond memories of my courtship of my wife, and also of the heavy-duty prescription cough syrup that used to be dispensed at the Williams College infirmary.

Although I generally don't approve of fruit juice after dark, the Bellini—Prosecco, the Italian sparkling wine, and peach juice—invented at Harry's Bar in Venice, is a beautiful starter, particularly if the peach juice is fresh. A champagne-based aperitif, the kir royale, has caught on here in the States, although I seem to remember hearing more calls for it in the 1980s. It consists of several dashes of cassis added to a glass of champagne. The tart acidity of the champagne and the sticky fruit of the cassis establish the right tension. The plain, still-wine version is best when the wine base is something tart, like Sauvignon Blanc or Aligoté from Burgundy.

Currently, my favorite aperitif is Lillet, which has been concocted in the Bordeaux region at the edge of Sauternes since 1887. It enjoyed a great vogue in this country after the Second World War, and again in the mid-1980s among the kinds of folks who play croquet and whose pictures appear in *W.* The new and improved version of this predinner quaff deserves a wide audience, particularly among those who appreciate wine. Best known in its original *blanc* incarnation, it also comes in a sangria-like *rouge.* Both are made from Cru Bourgeois Bordeaux wine, which is goosed with the addition of ten fruit liqueurs and aged for a year in wood.

The Lillet factory is located in the middle of the small, trafficky town of Podensac; once you turn off the main drag into the fruit-scented somnolence of the factory's courtyard, you feel you have left behind the era of internal combustion. The wooden buildings are embellished with the original Victorian gingerbread tracery and further decorated with colorful Art Nouveau and Art Deco Lillet posters, some of which display the spelling *Lilet.* (The name of the founding family, Lillet, is pronounced "lee-lay," but over the years there was concern that the home team, as is the French way, when confronted with a double *L,* would pronounce it "lee-yay," thereby possibly baffling le bartender.)

In 1985, after nearly a century producing the zingy aperitif, the Lillet family sold it to Bruno Borie, himself the scion of the distinguished Bordeaux family that owns Château Ducru Beaucaillou and several other important properties. Borie had always loved Lillet, but he hired an oenologist from the University of Bordeaux to help him refine the original product; the tweaking has tended to make Lillet more vinous and less spirituous. (The alcohol level is 17 percent, far lower than that of the average cocktail.) Borie has improved the base wine; tasted before it is blended, the Sémillon he uses is very pretty on its own. The exact recipe is secret, although several kinds of citrus peel are involved, as well as something called cinchona bark that provides the bitter counterpoint so important in a good aperitif. The underlying sweetness makes it, like the sweet wines of neighboring Sauternes, an excellent (and less expensive) accompaniment to foie gras and Roquefort.

Borie likes to serve Lillet chilled, on the rocks, with a slice of orange or lemon or both. (Which means if you happen to be an American in France, for once in your life you can demand ice in your drink without feeling crass.) And as a final grace note he squeezes an orange peel into the flame of his cigarette lighter, spraying the drink with flaming orange oil, a trick that can provide a useful diversion if you have kids hanging from your limbs during the cocktail hour; although this aperitif probably tastes best when you're temporarily childless, standing on the terrace of Borie's eighteenth-century château in Saint-Julien, looking out over the vineyards at the end of a hot October day, contemplating the meal and the wines to come.

CLIFF NOTES FROM THE CELLAR

The next best thing to knowledge is the appearance of knowledge. I know from personal experience that it takes years of reading, tasting, attending tedious multilingual dinners, freezing one's ass off in cold cellars, and nursing headaches to become a certified wine bore. What many of us want is the ability to impress our friends, and especially our enemies, and to be able to spend our money in such a way as to certify our connoisseurship. In that spirit I offer the following Cliff Notes on wine appreciation. These ten rules have taken me half a lifetime to collect, but I offer them as a public service. Master them and you will be able to operate a wine list with dexterity or plan the liquid part of an impressive meal.

1. Avoid artichokes whenever you consume wine. They contain an acid called cynarin, which makes wine taste sweet. Not as bad, but still dangerous, is asparagus, which contains phosphorous and mercaptan, turning most wines ugly. If you are planning a dinner party with wines, leave out these foods. Ditto soup and salad—they are almost impossible to match with wine. If you are at Daniel or Ducasse and you are ordering the tasting menu, tell the chef to skip these foods when he asks if there is anything you don't eat. Turn to your fellow diners and mutter, "Wine killers."

2. Every five years there's a great worldwide vintage, most recently '85, '90, and '95. Almost every wine region in the world experienced good to outstanding vintages in these years, the '95s being most relevant at the moment, since they are most readily available. However . . .

3. Beware of famous Euro vintages in their youth. For more expensive French (and some Italian) wines, one of the criteria for supposed greatness is the ability to improve with age, which means the wines have an abundance of bitter tannin and acid, and hence may well taste offensive when young (and even when they are old, for that matter). I recently had two vintages of the J. L. Chave Hermitage on successive nights. The first night I had the '88, a "great" vintage. Unfortunately, it wasn't nearly ready to drink, requiring another five years or so to shed its nasty, mouth-puckering tannins. The next night I had the '92—

supposedly a lousy vintage. But the wine was wonderful—fruity and perfectly integrated, despite its far cheaper price and a mediocre score from Robert M. Parker Jr. Right now the lowly '93 Bordeaux is probably more fun to drink than the far more highly rated, but tannic, '95. A corollary to this rule is that great makers almost always make good wine, no matter what the vintage.

4. Almost any zinfandel that starts with *R* is good. For instance, Ridge, Rafanelli, Ravenswood, Rabbit Ridge, Rosenblum, Renwood. Ditto any zin that ends in *elli*. Like Martinelli. We speak of red zinfandel, of course. About white zinfandel, the proper attitude is a lip-curling condescension. The word *puhleaz* should be uttered.

5. Any Italian wine that ends in the letters *aia* is very good indeed. This seems to be the result of the fame of Sassicaia, the so-called Super Tuscan Cabernet. Today you can count on Ornellaia, Solaia, Lupicaia, Brancaia, Tassinaia, and Piastraia. I don't know why, but they are all wonderful.

6. There's no such thing as bad champagne. Unless of course, it's been badly shipped or stored. By *champagne*, I mean the stuff that comes from the region of that name in north-central France and is imported to the States. The bad ones don't seem to get sent here. There are perfectly decent sparkling wines from other parts of the world, but why bother when you can get the real thing—a nonvintage brut—for twenty to thirty bucks? Just for fun, order one that no-body, including you, has ever heard of. Like J. Lassalle or Henri Germain.

7. Burgundy should follow Bordeaux. And Pinot Noir should follow Cabernet Sauvignon. This advice flies in the face of the conventional wisdom to follow lighter wines with heavier wines. But I've found that the sweet fruit of Pinot Noir tends to make the more rugged Cabernet taste bitter. (Merlot-based Bordeaux from Pomerol and Saint-Émilion are the exceptions to this rule.)

8. Almost everybody likes Chardonnay, and California Chardonnay—in almost any price range—is the most idiot-proof wine in the world. Not necessarily subtle. But like Harrison Ford, it gets the job done. Wine snobs love to bash it, though you can have it both ways by saying to your guests, "It's become fash-ionable to dump on Chardonnay, but we think this Casa New Oak is hard to beat." Viognier is way cooler, but you have to know what you're doing.

9. White wine with fish, red with flesh is a pretty reliable rule. But any idiot can follow rules—it's far cooler to break them. Pinot Noir can be great with salmon, particularly grilled salmon. (The oily flesh highlights the bright Pinot fruit.) And sweetish German Riesling is always good with pork and/or veal. If someone else is buying Château Pétrus or Château d'Yquem, by all means drink as much of it as you can, no matter what the hell you're eating. Give the food to the dog.

10. Finally, the rule I call Don't try this at home: I love red and white Burgundy only slightly less than I love my children. But unless you are prepared to misspend a year or two of your life in study, and thousands of dollars, stay the hell away from the Côte d'Or, the source of more heartbreak and tears than country-music radio. Leave it to the experts, baby.

SPECIAL BONUS RULE: If you are called upon by a waiter or sommelier to pronounce judgment on a wine, trust your palate. If it tastes nasty, send it back. If it tastes okay but you feel inclined to make some judgment, say, "Needs a little time in the glass."

HOW TO START YOUR OWN NAPA VALLEY WINERY WITHOUT REALLY TRYING

So you just took your Internet company public. You've got your house in Atherton and your ski lodge in Jackson Hole. You've got your Perini Navi yacht and as for wings, you probably opted for the slightly geeky Canadair over the flashy Gulfstream V. What you really want now is your own custom Napa Valley boutique winery. Portfolio candy. Just a thousand cases a year of super-concentrated cab that Robert M. Parker Jr. will score in the high nineties *and* that will instantly become impossible to find in the marketplace. Like Bryant Family Vineyard or Colgin Cellars or Screaming Eagle. A cool minimalist label with your name on it, or maybe the name of your boat. So who you gonna call?

You might start with the Napa Wine Company. "We get two or three calls like that a week," says Rob Lawson, the genial general manager of the venerable firm at the crossroads of the one-horse town of Oakville, right smack in the middle of the Napa Valley. More than sixty different labels, including such giants as—well, actually, we're not supposed to mention any names—avail themselves of some aspect of Napa Wine Company's services, from grape crushing to bottle labeling. But the most interesting aspect of the business is the custom-crush operation, whereby Napa provides wine making facilities and services to twenty-five boutique labels that are too small to justify the multimillion-dollar capital expenditure of constructing their own winery. Among them are some of the most famous cult labels in California, including Bryant, Colgin, Pahlmeyer, and Staglin Family Vineyard.

The Napa Wine Company was founded in 1877 at the start of the first California grape rush. The facility has been owned since 1993 by the Pelissa family, who have been growing grapes in Napa since the turn of the century. Theoretically, one could buy five or six tons of Cabernet grapes from the family and then truck them over to Napa Wine Company, where managing partner Andrew Hoxsey, a Pelissa on his mother's side, would be waiting in his Panama hat, a well-cut tweed jacket over jeans, and ostrich cowboy boots. If you were very lucky—and flush—you might have been able to hire one of the top-gun blond winemakers, like Helen Turley (of Marcassin, Bryant, Colgin, Pahlmeyer fame) or Heidi Barrett (Grace Family Vineyards, Screaming Eagle), who would already have overseen the sorting of grapes in the vineyard and who would now be on hand to help load them onto the conveyor belt for additional sorting before they are decanted into the state-of-the-art Delta destemmer, where they are divorced from their astringent stems and then pumped into a stainless-steel fermenting tank. Without going into all the details, let's just say that Helen or Heidi would, in exchange for a princessly retainer, provide Napa Wine Company with a winemaking protocol and supervise the successive stages of pressing, pumping the free run and press juice into new oak barrels (six hundred dollars apiece and up), and racking (pumping the wine out of the barrels to remove sediment). Napa Wine Company would bottle this juice, after fourteen or eighteen months in new French oak barrels, and slap the label of your choice on it. Casa McInerney, say, or something equally euphonious.

Jayson Pahlmeyer, a bon vivant and former San Francisco–based lawyer who looks amazingly like a youthful Buck Henry and who entertains like Diamond Jim Brady, was someone who had the dream. Fortunately for Jayson, he started pursuing it in the mid-1980s, when there were still a few prime undeveloped vineyard sites in the valley and Turley was still serving her apprenticeship at B. R. Cohn Winery, back in the days before her entry into a Calistoga restaurant could provoke a reverential hush, and before her consulting fee could finance an expedition to the South

Pole. From 1993 to 1999 Helen made Pahlmeyer's Chardonnay, Merlot, and Bordeaux blend wines at the Napa Wine Company. Her methods, especially her practice of bottling wines unfiltered, were initially considered so radical and risky that she was asked to sign a waiver absolving the company of liability for whatever the results might be. (Most high-end winemakers now avoid filtration; the result has been more flavorful wines despite the risk of spoilage from yeasts and bacteria.) Helen also made her own heroic Marcassin Chardonnay and the cult Cabernet Colgin there until recently. She continues to make the celestial Bryant Family on the premises though she left Pahlmayer in '99. (Winemaking responsibility for Colgin has now been taken over by her former protégé at Peter Michael, Mark Aubert.) Pahlmeyer still shows up at some retail outlets around the country. Most of Turley's wines are available only by mailing list, although they usually turn up at auction a few months after release for five or six times the release price.

Another beneficiary of the custom-crush operation is Andrew Hoxsey himself, who—like that Hair Club for Men guy—has become his own client, starting his own boutique Napa Wine Company label with fruit from his family vineyards. Presently, he's producing small quantities of Cabernet Sauvignon, Sauvignon Blanc, and Pinot Blanc. The wines are made by Randy Mason, who also makes a very fresh, fruit-packed Sauvignon Blanc under his own name at the winery. Mason is one of twenty-five so-called alternating proprietors who are bonded under the umbrella of the Napa Wine Company.

No matter how much you sell your software company for, you'll have to wait at least a year or two to become an alternating proprietor at NWC. They're booked solid. Not to mention the fact that premium Cabernet grapes are becoming hard to find, even at four thousand dollars a ton. And don't get too hot and bothered about Helen Turley. At this point she needs new clients like she needs winemaking lessons; she recently dumped an eager prospect when he had the bad manners to take a cell call in a local restaurant.

VITICULTURE 101

Daniel Roberts reckons he's dug more than eleven thousand holes in the course of his professional life. A big, pro-wrestler-sized guy in his fifties, Roberts looks like he could dig a pit with his bare hands, but he generally uses a backhoe for the first part of the job. Once the hole is deep enough, he likes to climb in and get his hands dirty. Roberts is in charge of soil management at Kendall Jackson. Watching him crumbling, sniffing, and even tasting a clump of loam in his hands, you know that this is a labor of love. Around the Napa Valley he's known as Dr. Dirt.

Roberts, who studied agronomy at the University of New Hampshire, says that his mother once told him he was so dirty he ought to get a doctorate in it. He did, and lately the California wine industry is beginning to get down with him. "For years," he says, "California focused on what was above ground." Now Golden State winemakers are starting to suspect what the French have known for years—that dirt is important, and that the character of a wine is largely determined in the vineyard.

Taking me on a tour of a hillside Cabernet vineyard that will become a source for Jess Jackson's boutique Cardinale cab, Roberts shows me three test pits that have successively richer and less rocky soil, and then points out how the vines adjacent to the lowest hole are more vigorous and unkempt. In fact, the lower part of the vineyard is too lush for his taste—"rocks are good for cab"—which is why, when it's replanted, he will order a less vigorous rootstock for this part of the vineyard.

Roberts is part of an informal fraternity of California viticulturalists who are shifting the focus of winemaking from the cellar to the vineyard itself. Small, dirt-conscious wineries like Saintsbury in Carneros, which lack the awesome resources of Kendall Jackson (aka the Evil Empire), avail themselves of the services of vine-wrangler-for-hire Martin Michizuki, who carries his pruning shears holstered on his hip. The boyish, taciturn Michizuki supervises viticulture for Saintsbury owners David Graves and Richard Ward, two U.C. Davis grads. Michizuki, who was born in Fresno, came to viticulture by way of a degree in entomology from Berkeley, although fortunately no one seems to call him Dr. Bugs.

(His face does light up, though, when he points out a vine damaged by the nasty phylloxera louse—like someone recognizing an old friend.) Graves and Ward have been producing very good Pinot Noir in Carneros for more than a decade, about half of that from purchased grapes. But their quest for a Grand Cru American Pinot Noir led them to start over, literally from the ground up. Seven years ago they found what they considered an ideal site in Carneros—the Brown Ranch, just a couple of miles from their winery. In conjunction with Michizuki they conducted extensive soil and drainage tests and began the laborious process of marking out different "blocks" and choosing the rootstocks best suited to each.

Short Viticulture 101 interlude: Prior to the nineteenth century, grapevines were planted on their own roots, like most sensible members of the vegetable kingdom. Since the mid-eighteenth-century phylloxera epidemic, European varietal grapevines (cab, Pinot, Chardonnay, et al.) are always grafted onto louse-resistant American rootstocks. Just to complicate matters ridiculously further, the aboveground vine material is generally cloned from a single mother vine. Growers have many clones to choose from. Custom viticulture thus involves hundreds of possible combinations of clone and rootstock. The first two vintages of Saintsbury Brown Ranch Pinot Noir show that meticulous matchmaking of soil type to plant material can have a hugely beneficial impact on wine quality.

"To make a certain quality of wine, you have to grow your own grapes," insists John Wetlaufer, business partner and husband to "wine goddess" Helen Turley. "It's totally artificial," he says, "to separate grape growing and winemaking." Over the years, while Helen became the most sought-after winemaker in California, Wetlaufer began to specialize in the agricultural side of the biz. A natural scholar who looks like he should be teaching at Berkeley (he studied philosophy and the history of science), Wetlaufer became a self-taught viticulturalist by reading everything he could find and visiting the best Pinot and Chardonnay vineyard sites in California.

After years of consulting for operations like Pahlmeyer, and of purchasing grapes (and fighting with growers) for their own Marcassin Chardonnay, Wetlaufer and Turley finally bought their dream site, a southeast-facing slope on the second ridge in from the Pacific in western Sonoma. "The first aspect of viticulture is site selection," John tells me as we walk the steep, rocky rows of the bleakly beautiful vineyard. The second aspect, development, involves dozens of backhoe pits. Like his pals at Saintsbury, Wetlaufer mapped out blocks and laboriously matched them with rootstocks and clones, mostly in the interest of lowering vigor (grape quality and quantity being inversely related). He spaced and positioned the rows to optimize the exposure to sunlight.

What happens above ground is equally important. Grapevines, like children, need discipline and boundaries; the Marcassin vines are meticulously trained and pruned till they resemble green solar panels. Although

Burgundy was once his model, Wetlaufer believes that standard Burgundian canopy management promotes vines that are basically too short and too fat to allow optimum ripening. "The goal," he says, "particularly with red grapes, is to get direct light on the fruit in the morning, but not the hotter afternoon sun." Every leaf in the vineyard is accounted for. "We're looking for fifteen to seventeen leaves per shoot, and that will ripen one or two bunches." Rampant greenery is discouraged. "The vine allocates carbohydrates between fruit and vegetation." Too much greenery robs the fruit of rootborne nutrients. Wetlaufer speaks of grape leaves as if they are at best a necessary evil. Recently Wetlaufer and his pal Dr. Dirt have gotten into computer modeling of terrain and Global Positioning System satellite technology. He tried to explain it to me on the long drive back down the Pacific coast, past the herds of seals at the mouth of the Russian River, but after four or five hours of Viticulture 101 my head was aching. Science is not my strong suit. Fortunately, after the long drive back to civilization, I got to taste Marcassin in the presence of the wine goddess herself. Moving from her '98 Gauer Ranch Chardonnay, made with purchased grapes, to the '98 Chardonnay from her own vineyard was a revelation. The first was spectacular. The second, made by the same winemaker employing the same cellar techniques, was even better, almost beyond superlatives.

"That's viticulture," said Helen, tipping her glass to her husband.

WHAT TO DRINK
WITH CHEESE

A year ago, through no virtue of my own, I found
myself dining at Pierre Gagnaire, one of Paris's newest
and hottest three-star restaurants. The food is wildly
inventive—an appetizer called simply *pomme de terre*
contained some half-dozen ingredients, including foie
gras, along with a single bite of cheesy mashed potato.
After the extravaganza of the first two courses, I
wanted to finish simply, with some cheese. Our bottle
of Volnay being empty, I decided to order a half bottle
of something for the cheese. Red, naturally. Claret,
probably, in the English tradition. The sommelier sized
me up as if trying to decide whether I was worth educating. Gently, he steered me toward the white side of
the wine list, informing me that the bulk of cheeses on

offer would go far better with, say, a Vouvray, or a white Burgundy, which is what I eventually selected. And damned if he wasn't right.

Six months later, at the two-star Enoteca Pinchiorri in Florence, the sommelier pointed to my unfinished 1995 Lafon Meursault, a white Burgundy, when I asked him advice on a wine for the cheese. And as if these two experiences weren't enough to confound the orthodoxy of drinking red wine with cheese, I sat down with my kids recently to steal some of their macaroni and cheese and discovered that the cheap Chilean Chardonnay I was sipping was a near-perfect match. These experiences have led me to question the widespread assumption that cheese calls out for red wine only.

The cheese course, served at the end of the meal— as opposed to that plate of Brie and Cheddar that still precedes many American meals and poetry readings— is just beginning to catch on in this country, a late manifestation of our culinary revolution. It can be either a supplement or an alternative to dessert. Everybody agrees that cheese goes well with that other product of controlled decomposition, namely wine, though some of the same people who demand warning labels on wine bottles will also tell you that cheese is bad for your health. To which my answer is: "How many fat French alcoholics do you know?"

Max McCalman is skinny enough to impersonate a flagpole, despite the fact that he eats more cheese than anyone I know. (His diet tip: Skip the bread and crackers.) Max is the maître fromager ("cheese nut" *en anglais*) at Manhattan's Picholine restaurant, possibly the only one in this country. Max is the kind of guy who can detect "the western Welsh vegetation and the sea salt" in a slab of Llangloffan. Despite his deadpan Deputy Dawg demeanor, Max is as passionate about his field as any grape nut I've ever met. He thinks Reblochon is kind of wimpy. (Don't even talk to him about Brie.) And unlike the USDA, he believes that pasteurization, far from being a great boon to mankind, is actually weakening the species by reducing our exposure, and hence lowering our resistance, to various bacteria. When it comes to matching food and wine, which comprises the better part of his duties as a maître fromager, he is uncharacteristically cautious. "It's hard to find hard-and-fast rules," he admits.

Like most cheese nuts, Max finds that veined cheeses tend to go with fortified wines. Stilton and port is the classic combination that comes to mind, as well as Sauternes and Roquefort. "Basically, wine and cheese matching is a kind of balancing act," he says, and in these matches the saltiness of these cheeses finds its foil in the sweetness of the wines. In many cases, neither he nor I would advise risking the remains of a fine bottle of old Bordeaux or Burgundy on any of the blue cheeses.

Some of the great wine and cheese combinations are regional; it's hard to find a better match than Sancerre and Crottin de Chavignol (a chèvre), which are both from the Loire Valley. This pairing can be extended beyond the region: Most goat cheeses seem to go well with young Sauvignon Blanc. Again, it's a question of balance—in this case, of pH levels. The high acidity of the Sauvignon Blanc seems to cut through the chalky alkalinity of the chèvre. Or something like that. Yet another regionally inspired white wine and cheese combo—this one originating in Alsace—is Muenster and Gewürztraminer.

As the sommelier at Pierre Gagnaire suggested, white Burgundy seems to be a versatile cheese wine, although Max cautions against the average oaky California Chardonnay. The mineral quality of a Puligny or a Meursault or even a Chablis seems to wed especially well with the earthiness of Gruyère, which is a feisty partner for most other wines.

Red wine definitely has a place at the cheese board, but, with apologies to my English friends, I'm convinced that the mellow charms of old Bordeaux and Burgundy are lost in the company of any but the mildest cheeses. A certain amount of acid, tannin, and young fruit helps a red wine keep up its end of the conversation with a hunk of fermented milk. Reblochon is one of the few good accompaniments to a red Burgundy. And one cheese that seems to me to cry out for red wine is Cheddar. In its aged English form— from Neal's Yard Dairy, for instance—it's the Platonic form of curd. A good Cheddar seems to be friendly enough to get along with a variety of red wines, including younger, burlier Cabernets (or Bordeaux) and Rhône reds like Châteauneuf-du-Pape and Côte-Rôtie.

If you've got a really complex, expensive bottle of wine open, it's probably best to keep the cheese simple; in this regard, a good Cheddar at the end of a meal serves the same function as an unadorned leg of lamb. But let's not get too geeky about all of this: As often as not, whatever wine is left on the table will taste fine with whatever cheese you have on hand.

WHAT GOES WITH TURKEY?

My father went through a period of drinking bourbon old-fashioneds with Thanksgiving dinner. His was the cocktail generation. On my eighteenth Thanksgiving under his roof, he showed me the recipe: one teaspoon of sugar, several dashes of Angostura bitters, one tablespoon of hot water, and a shot or two of bourbon. The maraschino cherry was optional. Perhaps the picture of the turkey on the bottle inspired this particular match. The problem with hard liquor, of course, is that it tends to be highly combustible, often leading to conflagrations at family gatherings, or at least at ours: I seem to remember a certain amount of weeping, shouting, recrimination, and gnashing of teeth. *Long Day's Journey into Night* kind of stuff.

Which can be particularly awkward for visiting lovers and foreigners. I gave up drinking Thanksgiving old-fashioneds shortly after I started, and ever since I have been experimenting with vinous lubricants for the big dry bird of the Pilgrims.

Let's begin with a caveat: There is no perfect solution, no sublime match made in heaven à la oysters and Chablis, Yquem and foie gras. While turkey is something of a tabula rasa, the traditional accompaniments—cranberries, yams, stuffing, et al.—complicate the flavor-matching equation considerably. Which gives a certain amount of freedom: You can pick your favorite color—white, pink, or red—and work from there.

At the risk of sounding like I'm wimping out, I would always recommend champagne. First, because it's *the* wine for special occasions, and second, because it has the acidity to stand up to those candied yams. Last Thanksgiving I was very happy with Krug's undated Grande Cuvée, a big baritone of a champagne, which, with its dried-fruit flavors and leaf-pile nose, always tastes to me like autumn in a glass. The '95 Veuve Clicquot and Bollinger Grande Année are two excellent, sort of affordable choices. Rosé champagne—made with 10 percent still, red wine—has a little more depth of flavor than the white stuff, and that can come in handy when you have a mouthful of relatively bland bird. And it looks good—even more festive than regular champagne. If by any chance you are coming to my house for Thanksgiving, I would recommend that you bring a bottle or two of the sublime '88 Dom Perignon Rosé (two hundred dollars).

If you don't want bubbles, one of the best Thanksgiving white wines comes to us via Alsace, where white wines have to stand up to a hearty Germanic cuisine. Gewürztraminer, with its exotic, spicy flavors, is my favorite Thanksgiving white wine. Even when vinified dry, it always seems slightly sweet and nicely complements the sweeter side dishes of Thanksgiving. Gewürztraminer is not for the faint of heart; those who are freaked out by the zany South Sea flavors—litchi nuts, rotting pineapples—might do better with a half-dry *(halbtrocken)* German Riesling or, if you'd rather buy American, Bonny Doon's inexpensive Pacific Rim Riesling. The only really good American example of Gewürz I have tasted comes from Martinelli Vineyards, best known for its legendary Jackass Hill zinfandel, which, come to think of it, I may drink this Thanksgiving if I can manage to lay my hands on any. With its bold fruit and peppery grace notes, zinfandel is one of the best red-wine solutions to turkey and a spicy dressing. Red zin is definitely the patriotic choice, since, like the turkey— which Ben Franklin proposed as the national bird—it is an American invention. As a rule of thumb, any zin that starts with an *R* seems to be good: Rafanelli, Ridge, Rabbit Ridge, Renwood, Ravenswood, Rosenblum, et al.

Rather than wrestling their turkey to the ground and clubbing it with a big red zin, certain well-trained palates prefer to romance it with Pinot Noir or Burgundy. Burgundy works best if you go light on the sweet side dishes and heavy on the cash. The Côte d'Or is legendarily confusing, but Jadot and Drouhin are almost always reliable. The best news in recent years from the Côte d'Or is the resurrection of Bouchard Père et Fils, one of the largest producers, which under new ownership is finally living up to its massive potential. Look for its Premier Cru Volnays and Beaunes in particular.

Thanksgiving coincides with the much ballyhooed release of Beaujolais Nouveau, which must be why people keep telling me it's a great Thanksgiving quaff. Or maybe it's because it's the liquid equivalent of yams with lots of marshmallows on top. Whatever you choose to wash down your turkey with, try to remember that if you hear yourself whining that your parents loved your brother more than they loved you, you've probably consumed too much.

HALF NOTES

Tragically, my wife doesn't drink wine, except when she is confronted with a glass of Château d'Yquem. Even when she doesn't see the label, she has the good taste to love the king of Sauternes. Recently, at a friend's birthday party, she innocently asked the waiter for another glass of the delicious dessert wine. Since the bottle was empty, the waiter obligingly fetched another—it happened to be a '53 Yquem—and opened it. The host gallantly bit his tongue—to the bleeding point, no doubt—the bottle probably costing far more than his wife's new Marc Jacobs beaded dress. Though Sauternes was often drunk with every course in the nineteenth century, I can't afford to stock my larder with Yquem, and I can't seem to interest Helen in splitting a bottle of mere Burgundy or Bordeaux over dinner, no matter how often I explain to her that moderate drinkers have longer life expectancies, lower heart-attack rates, and a far lower incidence of rectal tightness. Hence my interest in half bottles.

I don't usually advocate half measures, believing that anything worth doing is worth doing all the way, and then some. However, I'm getting older, and drinking a bottle of wine every night is, as a general practice, more than my doctor advises. Some of my fondest wine memories involve half bottles: a Keatsian '53 Margaux served by Julian Barnes with a lunch of sautéed wild mushrooms at his home in Highgate; a Soundgardenish '94 Araujo Eisele Vineyard Cabernet Sauvignon consumed solo with lamb chops at the Wappo Bar Bistro in Calistoga, just a few miles from where the wine was made. Though I took no notes, I can still summon up the sensation of drinking these two wines, thanks in part to the clarity of mind I associate with half bottles.

Generally speaking, a bottle of wine yields about six glasses, a half bottle about three (unless you're pouring too high, as most waiters seem to do, in which case you miss out on the nose). Three glasses is just about the right dose for a moderate evening's dinner. Hence, a half bottle is perfect for solo dining or, as in my case, for dining with a nondrinker. Of course, there are various systems for preserving open bottles of wine: I sometimes open a 750-milliliter bottle and immediately pour half of it into an empty half bottle, corking it promptly. The half bottle reduces air contact, and thus retards spoilage, though only for a day or two. Baccarat, Riedel, and The Wine Enthusiast all make special half-bottle decanters for this purpose. And the Vacu Vin pump system supposedly removes the need for containers; available for about twenty bucks at most wine stores, it comes with a couple of rubber stoppers and a hand pump, which sucks the air out of unfinished bottles—again slowing oxidation and decay. Be advised that bouquet freaks, such as Al Hotchkin Jr. at New York's Burgundy Wine Company, are suspicious of all this suction, preferring the half-bottle method.

Basically, there's no question—half bottles are more desirable than any preservation system. If you can find them. Your average wine store will display eight or ten of them somewhere near the cash register, as if they were novelty items. And many winemakers don't want the hassle of separate bottling lines. But there's hope. "More and more producers are making half bottles," says Jean-Luc Le Du, sommelier at New York's celestial Restaurant Daniel. "It's a response to the way people live and eat now. People are traveling a lot, eating alone. Also, half bottles are perfect for multicourse meals. With two people dining, it's much easier to match half bottles to individual courses. You could have, say, a Savennières with a soup, a white Burgundy with the fish, and a Pinot Noir with the meat course, and at the end of the meal you've split a bottle and a half of wine, which seems about right." Of course, if it's a special occasion, you might want to order a half bottle of dessert wine as well.

On the other hand, Richard Geoffroy, the efferves-cent, brush-cut physician-turned-winemaker at Dom Pérignon, doesn't trust the way champagne ages or holds it bubbles in half bottles. So you won't be seeing any DP in halves. Sad, since half bottles of champers are extremely useful, although I have sometimes opened a half bottle only to find it flat. Bad enough if you've paid fifteen, let alone fifty. There's no question that splits—quarter bottles of champagne—seldom de-liver the right fizz. On the other hand, if you insist on a luxury cuvée in a smaller format—as you sometimes should—Krug makes a very handy half bottle of its big, woody multivintage, which sells for about half a C note.

Experts agree that half bottles age more rapidly than full ones, largely because the ratio of air to wine inside the bottle is nearly doubled. This can be a bless-ing when you are waiting for big vintages in big bottles to come around. That '94 Araujo I mentioned earlier was, surprisingly, approachable without a whip and chair, but it might have been savage in a larger format. At the other end of the scale, far from having acceler-ated into a grimace, the '53 Margaux I consumed with the author of *Flaubert's Parrot* was holding up nicely when I drank it some forty years after the harvest.

Most dessert wines are available in half bottles, which makes a rare *Trockenbeerenauslese* or an Yquem from a good vintage seem more affordable. Unless you frequently entertain eight or ten guests, half bottles of these sweet wines are more useful than the 750s. A glass per person is usually sufficient, although when you are serving Château d'Yquem you will find that your guests seldom decline a second glass. If my wife is coming to dinner, you may want to have a second bottle standing by. Or not.

THE BIG STUFF: MAGNUMS, JÉROBOAMS, SALMANAZARS, AND NEBUCHADNEZZARS

An image of the good life that remains fixed in my memory derives from a wedding I attended many years ago in southern Vermont. One of the guests, the best man, brought a Salmanazar of Pol Roger champagne, which seemed to me an incredibly stylish and extravagant gift. I can still see him, his tuxedo silhouetted against the white clapboard of the eighteenth-century farmhouse, staggering around the lawn with the giant green bottle in his arms, aiming it at our outstretched glasses, dousing sleeves and shoes with the overflow. I had never heard before of a Salmanazar—which contains nine liters—nor of Pol Roger champagne. But I have remembered both names ever since, unlike those of the bride and groom.

Sometimes size matters. Big bottles are inherently festive, tokens of celebration and abundance. Like luxury cuvée champagne or first-growth Bordeaux, they make a statement: something along the lines of "This is an occasion and we're going to have some serious fun." Or even "Partay!"

The standard wine bottle has been pretty consistent in size for centuries. Now fixed in most countries at 750 milliliters, the volume was probably based on the lung capacity of the average glassblower back when bottles were handblown. According to the *Oxford Companion to Wine,* "The bottle has in its time been described as a suitable ration of wine for one person at a sitting, one person per day, and two people at a sitting." Clearly, the 750-milliliter bottle is a useful format. But the magnum, which at one and a half liters is equivalent to two bottles, is widely regarded as the best size for bottle-aging late-blooming wines like Bordeaux. The thinking here is that wine in larger bottles ages more slowly than in smaller bottles, because aging is a process of oxidation, and the amount of oxygen in the neck of a regular bottle and a magnum is about the same although the volume of wine in the magnum is twice as great. Theoretically the magnum should age about half as fast as the standard bottle, which is not necessarily good if you are impatiently waiting for your clarets and cabs to overcome their awkward, snarly adolescence. But big bottles are great for extending the life of a serious wine and for fostering the nuances that can only come from thirty or forty years of bottle age. A few years ago I tasted the '61 Cheval Blanc in both standard format and magnum, and there was no question that the wine from the magnum was livelier and more complex.

I have to say I like big bottles for strictly superficial reasons—they're party-worthy and look good on the table. From the purely hedonistic point of view, if a magnum is good, a double magnum (four bottles, aka three liters) is better. If you are in refined company, of course, the term *double magnum* may sound a little excessive, evocative as it is of *Dirty Harry*–style weaponry. You may prefer the term *Jéroboam,* which sounds more sophisticated, more *je ne sais quoi,* and less like the prelude to a drunken orgy. The only problem is that the term *Jéroboam* applies to a three-liter bottle of Burgundy or champagne. But in Bordeaux the term is used for the four-and-a-half-liter bottle, which holds the equivalent of six regular bottles. On the other hand, if your party isn't quite large enough for a double magnum (or Jéroboam, as the case may be), you could try a Marie-Jeanne, which is equivalent to three bottles of Bordeaux, though it isn't produced for champagne or Burgundy. And I believe it's called a Big Gulp in California. Confusing? Hey, nobody said wine was easy. That's why I get paid the big bucks. Because I know where to find the chart below.

Capacity	Liters	Bordeaux	Champagne/Burgundy
2 bottles	1.5	magnum	magnum
3 bottles	2.25	Marie-Jeanne	not made
4 bottles	3	double magnum	Jéroboam
6 bottles	4.5	Jéroboam	Rehoboam
8 bottles	6	Impériale	Methuselah
12 bottles	9	not made	Salmanazar
16 bottles	12	not made	Balthazar
20 bottles	15	not made	Nebuchadnezzar

California generally follows the Bordeaux line, except in the three largest formats, although these are rarely produced. The humongous Nebuchadnezzar is seldom encountered. Quite aside from the difficulty of making the bottles, there is the question of how to pour from them; also, this format would probably be inappropriate for Jewish weddings, named as it is for the Babylonian king who dragged the Israelites back into captivity. The Balthazar is named for one of the three Magi and is almost as rare as an empty table at the Manhattan restaurant of the same name.

The most useful and available big format, of course, is the magnum. When, at a recent dinner, I put a mag of '94 Pahlmeyer Chardonnay on the table, I was rewarded with many queries and comments even before the guests had tasted it. The next morning I couldn't understand what had happened to the empty bottle until one of my guests sheepishly called to confess that he had staggered off with it because he wanted to turn it into a lamp.

MILLENNIUM

My plans for celebrating the millennium were hatched at a dinner party in London in the late 1980s. The idea was to collect and, finally, to consume some of the world's greatest wines over dinner as the century turned. Just about every other aspect of my life changed in the intervening years, but the plan survived—although in the end we started two weeks late and carried on for eight days.

The prime mover in this event was Julian Barnes, the celebrated English novelist, whom I first met in 1985. We shared an editor, and quickly discovered that we also shared an interest in wine. Barnes's oenophilia was far more advanced than my own: I was ignorant enough to be disappointed when, on my first visit to his London home, I saw that he was serving Châteauneuf-du-Pape rather than claret. Till I tasted the wines. The '62 and '67 Jaboulet Les Cedres we drank that night remain two of my fondest wine memories. I also discovered that Julian and his wife, literary agent Pat Kavanaugh, are great cooks. After that, although I lived three thousand miles from Tuffnel Park, I somehow managed to turn up for dinner at their home on a fairly regular basis.

The original millennial dinner plan was to drink wines rated a hundred points by Robert Parker—our guru. Later, we talked washing down a few courses with the '82 first growths from Bordeaux. Then Julian, a lover of Rhône wines, decided he wanted to include some of these. (Although the rap on Julian is that he's Appollonian and reserved even for a Brit, he tends to go for big, floozy, decadent wines.) Later still, I felt a patriotic compulsion to include California wines. Eventually we realized we'd need multiple dinners, with a hangover day—sorry, make that layover day—to accommodate our increasingly ambitious drinking plans. Not to mention the size of the guest list, which came to include wine critic Jancis Robinson and her husband, food writer Nick Lander; Auberon Waugh, the critic/curmudgeon/son of Evelyn; Simon Hopkinson, founding chef of Bibendum; and actor/comedian/ novelist Stephen Fry.

At the last minute the event was postponed due to apocalyptic millennial anxieties, and to the reluctance of my svelte and oenologically challenged wife, Helen, to celebrate the millennium, as she put it, "pigging out and talking about wine." The final plan was that we would have four dinners, the first of which would take place at Julian and Pat's home on my forty-fifth birthday on January 13. The last, also chez Barnes, would celebrate Julian's birthday on the 19th.

I was lucky enough to be born in 1955, a very good year in Bordeaux, which was the focus of the first dinner. Julian had been haunting the auction houses in recent years and had come up with a roster of incredible clarets. But first he opened a magnum of '76 Krug, a beautifully creamy, nutty champagne that helped ease the tension around the table. Matthew Evans, the publisher of Faber and Faber, had recently exchanged heated insults with fellow dinner guest Auberon Waugh on one of those BBC chat shows, and this was the first time they'd seen each other since. Literary London is like that. The truce initiated by the Krug was solidified with a '55 Lafite-Rothschild and a '55 Château Latour, served side by side. A kind of Laurel and Hardy pairing—the Lafite looking thin and pinkish, the Latour deep ruby and opaque. The Lafite was all foreplay—an incredible nose, like a really good cinnamon-based potpourri, but short and light on the palate. The Latour was fat, rich, full of fruit and earthy bass notes, the perfect wine for Julian's roast beef.

Pat, who's a bit of a gulper, had her cautionary sign set out in front of her, a piece of cardboard inscribed with the legend: NOT SO FAST. It didn't seem to slow her down. Waugh, a Tory and a contrarian by nature, loved the '55 Mouton-Rothschild, which came next, but it tasted pretty tight-assed to the rest of us, especially compared to the sweet, smoky, profound Cheval Blanc. It seemed impossible to improve upon until we took our first sips of the ambrosial '55 Château d'Yquem.

Two nights later the party resumed at the Hampstead home of Jancis Robinson and Nick Lander. The theme was California—I'd lugged most of the wines from the States over the previous few years. Looking very telegenic in Miyake, Jancis poured, dripping more wine than you might expect of one of the world's leading wine authorities. (Steady on, Jancis, that's a Prada shirt you just dribbled on.) We started with a white truffle risotto and a pair of Marcassin Chardonnays: the elegantly Puligny-like '93 Hudson Vineyard and the big floozy '94 Gauer Ranch. We then moved on to a shootout between two great cult Cabernets. First the '93 Harlan and Bryant Family, both huge and promising but shut down like a pair of grizzly bears in hibernation. The '94 Harlan and Bryant were more like a buff, gorgeous couple tanning on the beach. Opinions were divided as to the winners of these Harlan/Bryant face-offs—but the Brits were definitely impressed with this New World juice.

Nick's brilliant roast duck—cooked with star anise and some weird Thai tuber the name of which I forget—was already finished when we realized we had a final flight of reds, magnums of '94 Pahlmeyer Proprietary Red and '94 Pahlmeyer Merlot. Slackers might have thrown in the towel at this point, but we rolled up our sleeves and drank, judging the Merlot friendlier and flirtier, its sibling more complex and structured. Then Julian pulled out a '49 Château d'Yquem. Which was geographically heterodox, but hedonistically apposite—if anything, even more monumental than the '55 of the previous dinner.

The third dinner, cooked by master chef Simon "Hoppy" Hopkinson at his home, was supposed to have involved a vertical tasting of Jaboulet Hermitage La Chapelle from the 1960s and 1950s. That plan was scrapped when Julian, who was providing the wines, came down with an inner-ear problem. In his absence wine merchants Bill Baker and Steven Browett assembled a grab bag of great bottles, including a '61 Cristal, '68 "Y" from Château d'Yquem, and '71 and '88 Clos Saint-Denis from the great Domaine Dujac. Pat, who like her absent husband had never approved of Burgundy, actually requested a second glass of the '71, it was so good. (Though she'd brought her sign with her.) I brought a '78 Hermitage La Chapelle that will someday be great but at twenty-one years of age yielded all the pleasure of chewing an unshelled walnut. Most memorable was Simon's haricot verts with black truffles, or perhaps his veal roast.

Julian was still feeling a little shaky the morning of the 19th, his birthday. He perked up enough to eat a jumbo BLT at the Lord Palmerston, the pub around the corner, then lost vigor and conviction as the afternoon progressed. But as the first guests arrived, the sound of the cork on the '90 Cristal seemed to have a revivifying effect. Or perhaps it was the late arrival of the effervescent Stephen "Born to be Wilde" Fry, who drives a decommissioned black cab around town and is so polite that he's been known to take strangers to their destinations after they've jumped in the back.

Julian decanted the wines, which he insisted we taste blind. Perhaps I'm a genius, or perhaps I'm just familiar with Julian's taste, his cellar, and his generosity—I guessed the first wine as a thirty-something Cheval Blanc. (With its smoky, earthy notes, it might have been an Haut-Brion.) I proposed '64; Jancis took the prize by guessing '61. Whatever—it was one of the most perfect wines I've ever drunk. The following wines were also Cheval Blanc—'59, '53 and '49, the last being my other favorite, incredibly sweet, seductive, and spicy.

"How are you feeling?" I asked Julian sometime around 1956.

"I feel much better," he said—a case study for future research into the healthful properties of fine wine.

And that was even before he opened the '28 Yquem.

GLOSSARY OF SELECTED TERMS

Note: Generally speaking, European wines are named for the place they are grown (i.e., Bordeaux, Barolo) whereas New World wines are named for their grapes (i.e., Cabernet, Chardonnay).

appellation controlée. Short for *appellation d'origine controlée,* is France's prototype controlled appellation, her much-imitated system of designating and controlling her all-important geographically based names, not just of wines, but also of spirits such as Cognac, Armagnac, and Calvados, as well as certain food stuffs.

Barbaresco. Powerful red wine based on the Nebbiolo grape grown around the village of Barbaresco in the Piedmont region of northwest Italy. Long overshadowed by the wine of nearby Barolo, Barbaresco has emerged—thanks to the hyperkinetic Angelo Gaja—from Barolo's shadow to win recognition of its own striking qualities of elegance and aromatic intensity. Aka Gajaville.

Barolo. Perhaps the most powerful and dramatic expression of the Nebbiolo grape, this big red takes its name from the village of the same name nine miles to the south of the town of Alba in the region of Piedmont in northwest Italy. Barolos are known for their age-worthiness and for an aromatic quality often compared to "tar and roses."

Beaujolais. Incredibly picturesque, hilly region in east central France (also, the less incredible wine of that region). Most Beaujolais is red, made from the Gamay grape in a style that emphasizes the fruit and usually calls for early consumption. Often smells like bananas. Once upon a time it was, according to such authorities as Richard Olney, a very light, low-alcohol, food-friendly quaff, but the modern style calls for the addition of lots of sugar (chaptalization) to mimic hot vintages, creating a richer texture and flavor. For administrative purposes, Beaujolais is often included as part of greater Burgundy, but in terms of climate, topography, soil types, and even distribution of grape varieties, it's quite different. Aka Dobouefland.

Bordeaux. Important French port on the Garonne River leading to the Gironde estuary on the west coast. Bordeaux gives its name to the world's most famous wine region, which includes the vineyards of the so-called left bank—including the communes of Margaux, Saint-Julien, Paulliac, and Saint-Éstephe—as well as the smaller but increasingly prestigious right bank communes of Pomerol and Saint-Émilion, as well as lesser appellations.

Brunello di Montalcino. A powerful, backward red wine named for a strain of the Sangiovese grape (Brunello) particularly well adapted to the vineyards of Montalcino, a picturesque walled hill town in Tuscany in central Italy. Often considered one of the big three Italian reds, along with Barolo and Barberesco.

Burgundy. The most poignantly frustrating wine region on the planet, source of more heartache than country music radio. Known as Bourgogne in French (also the generic name for the wine of the region), this is the province of eastern France famous for its great red and white wines, produced mostly from Pinot Noir and Chardonnay grapes respectively. Burgundy includes the viticultural regions of the Côte de Nuits (north) and Côte de Beaune (south) in the department of the Côte d'Or—so named because of its (Oriental) east-facing aspect—as well as the Côte Chalonnaise and Mâconnais in the Saone-et-Loire.

Cabernet Sauvignon. The world's most renowned grape variety for the production of fine red wine. From its power base in Bordeaux, where it is almost invariably blended with other grapes, it has been taken up in other French wine regions and in much of the Old and New Worlds. Lately known as the signature varietal of the Napa Valley.

Chablis. The steely, dry white wine of the most northern vineyards of Burgundy in northeast France, named for the village. Made, like all fine white Burgundy, from the Chardonnay grapes. Paradoxically, however, in the New World, particularly in North America and Australia, the name Chablis has been borrowed and abused so that it is more often used to describe a dry white wine of uncertain provenance and no specific grape variety bearing no resemblance other than its color to true Chablis.

Chardonnay. Surely you don't have to ask. This white grape varietal successfully escaped botanical nomenclature to become a brand, a wine name familiar and popular as any to consumers. (There is a village of this name in Mâcon, though which came first we may never know.) In its Burgundian homeland, Chardonnay was for long the sole vine responsible for all of the finest white burgundy. In the late twentieth century, however, it was transplanted in most of the world's wine regions—where varietal labeling has become the norm—with such a high degree of success that Chardonnay was by the 1990s a name known to far more wine drinkers than Meursault or Montrachet.

Chianti. The name of a specific geographical area between Florence and Sienna in the central Italian region of Tuscany, as well as the tangy, dry red wines produced there. The Chianti zone is first identified in documents of the second half of the thirteenth century, which named the high hills between Baliaccia di Monte

Luco "the Chianti Mountains." Chianti Classico is a more rigorously defined area traditionally associated with the best wines. Almost a joke twenty years ago, Chianti has lately rebounded in quality.

Claret. What the English call the red wines from the Bordeaux region. The term is often used to refer to a particularly dry, austere style of Bordeaux—for instance, the 1988 vintage.

Côte-Rôtie. The so-called Roasted Slope, a small steeply hilly appellation in the far north of the northern Rhone. In the 1970s, the area and its wines was somewhat moribund, a rather isolated outpost well north of Tain where the major *négociants* and the famous Hermitage Vineyard are situated. One man, Marcel Guigal, is chiefly responsible for the recent renaissance of this zone. The red wines, made from the Syrah grape, are aromatic and long-lived.

Grand Crus. French for great growths, are those Crus judged superior in some way. The term represents the apex of the classification system in Burgundy and Alsace, but does not exist in Bordeaux.

Grüner Veltliner. The most commonly planted vine variety in Austria and grown elsewhere in eastern Europe. In 1992 this well-adapted variety was planted on more than a third of Austria's 58,000 ha/143,000 acres of vineyard, particularly in lower Austria, where it represents more than half of total white grape production.

Merlot. The black grape variety associated with the great wines of Saint-Émilion and Pomerol, Merlot is Bordeux's most planted black grape variety, and has been enjoying ridiculous popularity elsewhere.

négotiant. French term for a merchant and one used particularly of wine merchants who buy in grapes or wine, blend different lots of wine within an appellation, and bottle the result under their own label. Making a perfectly balanced blend from a number of imperfect parts is a potentially noble calling, but one that once provided so many opportunities for adulteration and fraud that it brought the entire profession into question, if not ill repute.

oenology. The knowledge or study of wine, derived from the Greek *oins,* meaning *wine.* The French and Italian terms are, respectively *oenologie* and *enologica.* Oenology has been used as synonymous with wine-making. There is a general tendency toward including the study of viticulture as well as wine production in the term, however, as more people accept that wine is made to a great extent in the vineyard.

Petite Sirah. A black grape variety that almost certainly originated in Europe though it's probably unrelated to the true Syrah (or to the grape that some French growers distinguish as a small-berry subvariety they call Petite Syrah). In other words no one knows how the hell it got to California, or from where, but many old vineyards are identified as such, and produce a powerful inky red wine.

Pinot Noir. A thin-skinned grape varietal responsible for red burgundy. Unlike Cabernet Sauvignon, which can be grown in all but the coolest conditions and can be economically viable as an inexpensive but recognizably Cabernet wine, Pinot Noir demands fanatical attention from both vine-grower and wine-maker.

Port. A fortified wine made by adding brandy to arrest fermenting grape—results in a wine, red and sometimes white, that is both sweet and high in alcohol. Port derives its name from Oporto (Porto), the second largest city in Portugal, whence the wine has been shipped for over 300 years by English merchants.

Pouilly-Fumé. One of the Loire's most famous wines—racy dry whites made from the Sauvignon Blanc grape. Not to be confused with Pouilly-Fuissée, which is made from Chardonnay and comes from Burgundy.

Premier Crus. First growths or premiers crus classes, are those crus judged of the first rank according to official regional classification. In Bordeaux, first is the highest designation based on the 1855 classification, while in Burgundy, premier is actually second to Grand Cru.

Riesling. The queen of white wine grapes (if Chardonnay is king). Vastly underappreciated in

America, this cold weather varietal reaches its greatest heights on the steep hillside Vineyards of Germany's Mosel Saar and Ruwer river valleys. France's Alsace region also produces great Riesling. Riesling has the capacity for great longevity. Its reputation in this century has been for sweetness; in fact, Riesling can be vinified to a mouth-puckering dryness, due to its high acidity. It also makes some of the world's greatest sweet wines, most notably German *eiswein*s and *trockenbeerenausleese*s.

Rosé. Wines colored any shade of pink, from hardly perceptible to pale red. For some reason they are rarely known as pink wines, although the English word *blush* has been adopted for particularly pale roses.

Sancerre. A hilltop town on the left bank of the upper Loire lends its name to one of the Loire's most famous wines: racy, pungent, dry white Sauvignon Blanc.

Sangiovese. Red grape variety that is Italy's most planted and is particularly common in central Italy. Main ingredient of the infamous Chianti. In 1990 almost 10 percent of all Italian vineyards were planted with some form of Sangiovese. Increasingly planted in California, with mixed results.

Sauternes. Perhaps the world's greatest sweet wine, made in the Bordeaux commune of that name. Usually a blend of Sauvignon Blanc and Sémillion, the characteristic honeyed sweetness derives from botrytis— a fungus that infects the grapes in autumn and concentrates their flavors.

Sauvignon Blanc. The varietal responsible for some of the world's most distinctive, dry white wines: Sancerre and Pouilly-Fumé from the Loire Valley are made exclusively from Sauvignon Blanc, which is also used along with Sémillon to make white Bordeaux. Increasingly planted in other parts of the world, it has done especially well in New Zealand.

Shiraz. The Australian (and South African) name for the Syrah grape, a name arguably better known by consumers than its Rhone original.

sommelier. Widely used French term for a specialist wine waiter or wine steward. The sommelier's job is to ensure that any wine ordered is served correctly and, ideally, to advise on the individual characteristics of every wine on the establishment's wine list and on food and wine matching.

Saint-Éstephe. The northernmost and most bucolic of the four important communal appellations in the Haut-Medoc district of Bordeaux. The wines have the historical reputations of being tough buggers, slow to evolve and show their charms.

Saint-Émilion. Important red wine district on the right bank of the Garonne River in Bordeaux. It takes its name from the prettiest town in the Bordeaux region by far, and one of the few to attract tourists to whom wine is of no interest. Merlot is the predominant grape here; the wines have a tendency to show their charms earlier than those of the left bank.   Once among the least glamorous appellations, Saint-Émilion has lately become the hottest commune of all, thanks to the cult appeal of the so-called *vins de garages* such as Valandraud.

terroir. Much discussed term denoting the total natural environment of any viticultural site. Location, location, location—with all that that entails, including geology and metereology. No precise English equivalent exists for the quintessentially French term and concept. It is the foundation of the French Appellation Controlée system—the reason the French name their wines after the site, rather than the grape.

varietal. Grape type, i.e., Cabernet Sauvignon, Chardonnay, Pinot Noir, etc. In the New World, wines are usual named for the varietal from which they are made.

Viognier. Almost unknown and extinct white varietal that became fashionable in the early 1990s. (See *Brightness Falls* [McInerney, 1992] for an early literary reference.) Once limited to the Rhone river valley slopes around the village of Condrieu and used to make the wine of the same name, it is increasingly planted elsewhere, with mixed results.

Volnay. Attractive village in the Côte de Beaune district of Burgundy's Côte d'Or, producing eponymous elegant red wines from Pinot Noir.

Zinfandel. An exotic black grape variety, possibly related to the Primitivo grape of Italy, cultivated
predominantly in California.   For years it was used in
red jug wines and later in the production of a rosé-like
or blush wine called White Zinfandel, which remains
wildly popular, although much derided by the cognes-
centi. The last two decades have seen the rise of
powerful new Zinfandel-based reds. Many of the vineyards are as much as a century old, resulting in wines of
great power and richness.

SELECTED BIBLIOGRAPHY

Gerald Ascher, *On Wine*. New York: Vintage, 1984.

———, *Vineyard Tales: Reflections on Wine*. San Francisco: Chronicle Books, 1997.

Michael Broadbent, *The Great Vintage Wine Book II*. London: Christies, 1991.

Clive Coates, *Côte d'Or: A Celebration of the Great Wines of Burgundy*. Berkeley, California: University of California Press, 1997.

Michael Dibdin, *A Long Finish: An Aurelio Zen Mystery*. New York: Pantheon, 1998.

Jacqueline Friedrich, *A Wine and Food Guide to the Loire*. New York: Henry Holt and Co., 1996.

Matt Kramer, *Making Senes of Burgundy.* New York: William Morrow, 1990.

James T. Lapsley, *Bottled Poetry: Napa Winemaking From Prohibition to the Modern Era.* Berkeley: University of California Press, 1996.

A. J. Liebling, *Between Meals: An Appetite for Paris.* New York: Farrar Strauss Giroux, 1959.

Kemit Lynch, *Adventures on the Wine Route: A Wine Buyer's Tour of France.* New York: Farrar Strauss Giroux, 1988.

Ed McCarthy and Mary Ewing-Mulligan, *Wine for Dummies* (2nd Edition). Foster City, California: IDG Worldwide, 1998.

Patrick Matthews, *The Wild Bunch: Great Wines from Small Producers.* London: Faber and Faber, 1997.

Richard Olney, *French Wine and Food.* Northampton, Massachusetts: Interlink Publishing Group, 1997.

———, Reflexions. New York: Brick Tower Press, 2000.

Robert Parker, Jr., *Bordeaux: A Comprehensive Guide to the Wines Produced from 1961 to 1997.* New York: Simon & Schuster, 1998.

———, *Wines of the Rhone Valley* (Revised and Expanded Edition). New York: Simon & Schuster, 1997.

Emile Peynaud, *The Taste of Wine: The Art and Science of Wine Appreciation* (2nd Edition) Translated by Michael Schuster. New York: John Wiley and Sons, 1996.

Sylvain Pitiot and Jean Charles Servant. *Les Vins de Bourgogne*. Paris: Presse Universitaires de France, 1997.

Gambero Rosso (editor), *Italian Wines* 2000. New York: Gambero Rosso Inc., 1999.

Jancis Robinson, *Vintage Timecharts*. New York: Wiedenfeld and Nicholson, 1989.

Jancis Robinson (editor), *The Oxford Companion to Wine*. New York: Oxford University Press, 1994.

Brian St. Pierre. *A Perfect Glass of Wine*. San Francisco: Chronicle Books, 1996.

Edward Steinberg, *The Making of a Great Wine: Gaja and Sori Sand Lorenzo*. New York: Ecco Press, 1992.

Tom Stevenson, *Christies World Encyclopedia of Champagne and Sparkling Wine Wine*. London: Appreciation Guild, 1999.

Auberon Waugh, *Waugh on Wine*. London, 1987.

Frederick S. Wildman, Jr., *A Wine Tour of France*. New York: William Morrow, 1972.

INDEX